Brand to Bucks

A No Nonsense Guide
To Building A
Six Figure Brand

Coleen Otero
Founder of the CEO Chick Network

All rights reserved. This book, or parts thereof, may not be reproduced in any form without permission.

Printed in the United States of America

Book Cover designed by: Adam I. Wade

ISBN: 978-1-7329815-6-0

Library of Congress Control Number: 2018968494

Copyright 2017 by Coleen Otero
www.ColeenOtero.com

DEDICATION

Special thanks to all my teachers, pastors, mentors and coaches who taught me the importance of developing my gifts and abilities.

To my amazing parents, Hopeton and Barbara Hall thank you for your continued support, Lord knows I could not have done this without you.

To Mr. Juan "Tony" Otero, my husband, my friend, my boss, Human ATM, and more I could not do this without your love, prayers and support.

To my sons, Mekai, Josiah, Ethan and John Judah, let this book be a reminder that you can do anything you set your mind too. Stay focused!

To my CEO Chick Coaches and Community, you continue to hold me accountable to be a greater leader, teacher and sister. I am so grateful for you! This organization is proof that God is mindful of his daughters in the marketplace.

Finally, to my amazing clients that trust my creative processes and skill sets, it is such an honor to be a part of watching your growth and development.

To those that purchase this workbook, thank you for your support and for investing in yourself. I know the tips and tools in this book will help you to develop a brand that is both authentic and prosperous! It is time to master, market and monetize your brand!

> "Successful people do what unsuccessful people are not willing to do. Don't wish it were easier; wish you were better."
> *- Jim Rohn*

> "Building your brand should be your mission and not a mistake."
> *- Coleen Otero*

Table of Contents

Prologue 1
Introduction 5
Your Story 11
    Power of Authentic Storytelling 12
    Three-Part Storytelling Module 16
    Get Others To Tell Your Story 19
    Be Different From Your Competitors: 21
    Benefits of Social Media 22
Your Style 28
    Personal Style 31
    Must Have Staple Pieces for Men 31
    Must Have Staple Pieces For Women 34
    Fashion Sense 38
Your Skills 44
    Skillsets Of The Successful 47
    Communicate Like A Pro 48
    Network Like A Pro 49
    Meeting Management Skills 53
    Personal And Professional Development 55
Your Stuff 60
    Media 66
    Who Are You Serving? 69
    Your Content Calendar 70
    What's The Budget? 71
    Products And Services 73
Your System 77
    Key Operational Systems: 78
    Your Marketing System 79
    Your Payment System 82
    Your CRM System 83
    Effective Backend Management System 88

Your Success	94
Show Me The Money	95
Multiple Streams Of Income	96
Disrupt The Market:	98
Develop Successful Habits For Life:	104
Establish Joint Venture Partnerships:	108
Brand Stages	111
Your Notes	113
Client Stories	118
What Clients Are Saying	123
About The Author	124

PROLOGUE

As a Beauty Expert, Brand Strategist, Entrepreneur, Mentor, Speaker, Wife, Mother, and more... I totally understand how important it is to create a brand that's transcendent.

In 2009, my family and I began to go through some of the toughest times. We lost 4 properties, 3 cars, 2 businesses, and even 'close friends', all over a five-year period. After our final short sale, we moved in with my parents for what was supposed to be 2 months... Two years later we finally were stable enough to move out. It was during that time I truly became the six-figure earning entrepreneur you see today.

God placed a fight in me to WIN in life! It's the same fight I use to push my clients into purpose, literally!

In 2010, months after having our third son our finances hit a new low. My husband was with a temp agency and income was inconsistent. We were living in the last property that was up for a short sale. It was our very first home we purchased as a married couple.

There wasn't room for anything above our basic necessities. Our date nights were spent in one of my favorite places, the bookstore. I would go to the business section and go thru books on branding, online marketing, etc.

Anything that could give me information to help our family out of this financial noose.

The saying, "necessity is the mother of invention," is flat out true! I began to use online marketing via social media to promote my beauty business, Your Beauty Xpert, LLC.

I showcased my work to book clients. I launched my own hair line in 2012 to increase my service dollars. I also would sell exotic jewelry pieces and designer handbags.

If I found good deals on items that fell into the scope of my beauty brand, I would purchase it and sell it for a profit.

It was during that time I picked up this quote, "I love it enough to sell it!" As time progressed my husband landed a great paying job working as tech support with a pharmaceutical company.

I kept working my craft while he worked his butt off at that job. He took as much over time as he could, I traveled the city styling client's hair and my parents helped us with the kids. The grind was something serious.

By 2014, with both joy and anxiety, we moved out into a beautiful 2 story town home! We saved enough to fully furnish it, cash and still had money in our savings for a rainy day. As my business began to gain more exposure, the calls came into work on the set of Bravo's reality show Thicker Than Water. Followed by my hairline, Pure Luxe, being featured by talent on Oxygen's Preachers of LA, to being called to style hair for Sherri Shepherd, from The View, for her live comedy set.

People would inbox me asking, who does your branding? Who does your social media? Who did your logo? A light bulb went off for me! At this time, I began helping people with their brand. I did this for years before ever promoting it publicly. I wanted to be sure this was something I wanted to do and secondly, something I enjoyed doing.

My first official client, Kenya Taylor of Virtuous Tees came to me after I spoke at a Vision Board Party for her church. A single mom, working and going to school full time with a t-shirt company making an additional $2,500 annually in sales.

After our sessions together, we came up with a marketing concept for her brand, developed her brands identity, and improved her merchandise quality and process.

Within 6-months, she began to turn her numbers around drastically! She went from selling single items to selling bulk items.

We marketed to women groups, religious organizations, and targeted positive community efforts such as Domestic Violence Awareness, Cancer Walks, Aids Awareness, you name it, we went for it!

This single working mother of 3, went from making $2,500 to earning an additional $19,000 in sales the following year. While she was still working full time and going to school. Kenya's family helped her, they turned a room in her home into their official work site and now she is taking her brand into boutiques.

I am a firm believer that if you are going to show up in the marketplace, you have got to show up correct. We must master the art of serving our customers with a brand promise that is consistent, creative, authentic, and excellent.

There are several components you must have in place to set yourself up for success. Whether you were like me, peeling back the pages of this book while standing in a bookstore, or if you purchased it.

As you move throughout this book, it is my intention to inspire and educate you. There will be moments I like to call B2B Breaks, where you are to take the time out to think about your brand and to answer the questions presented to you.

The questions do not come at the end of the chapter. They are interjected throughout the sections while the topic is fresh in your mind.

I have been writing this book for the last 2 and a half years, in fact, as we speak, I am tucked away in my Downtown Atlanta Apartment adding all my finishing touches and thoughts.

A single copy of this book was given to a special young lady in the spring of 2016. She approached me after I spoke at a Women Conference to over 500 women about the importance of developing their brand.

Her name is Lisa. She wanted to start a non-profit mentorship program for young ladies, and she did not know where to start. She signed up for my coaching services and I gave her a copy of this book.

The cover was totally different, and it looked more like a workbook. I walked Lisa through each chapter of the book in our sessions together. Would you believe it was a 9-month process!

Lisa had to research some of the questions. She had no idea how much went into running a business. She did not really give much thought to what was required to bring a group of young ladies together for her mentoring services.

At the end of our time together Lisa had a much clearer picture of what her vision looked like and the action steps it would take to get there.

I have been adding different life lessons and professional experiences to the pages of this book ever since I met Lisa. As my brand evolves and expands, I am compelled to teach others how very possible it is to create a brand that transcends, impacts our world, and brings in a life changing salary.

Brand to Bucks is designed to make you dig, to reflect, improve, adjust, and reassess your brand. Take the time to read through the content and answer the questions.

This is the guide to building your brand to assist you in mastering, marketing, and monetizing your creative abilities. I have extracted the principles learned from the 20 years of my professional and personal experiences in business and share them step by step for you to apply.

I am super excited about your success so let's begin!

Introduction

What is Branding? Before we get started with the first key to building a successful brand, I need you to understand what it is.

Branding is not a website, it is not a logo, it is not a building, or any object for that matter. It is not marketing, it is not sales, it is not so much what is seen AT FIRST.

It is what is FELT. I know that sounds deep, but it really is not. The brand is the essence or spirit of an organization. The brand is the promise, the principles, the moral beliefs, the DNA, if you will, of the company.

It is from that place your brand is conceived and your business is birthed. The success and longevity of your business greatly relies on your brand's impact and consistency.

I often tell my clients, "I am not interested in building a brand as much as I am in changing a culture."

Strong brands have the ability to influence and impact lives on a global scale. They break all the rules, they can connect people of different races, different financial backgrounds, and even conflicting lifestyles - all for one common purpose. Isn't that powerful?

Once you grab hold of your big idea and you are crystal clear about your brand, you are now ready to develop your business.

Remember your brand is an expression of your principles and your business reflects your practices.

Once you come up with a concept you might think your next step is to get a business card or to purchase a website, right? I would advise otherwise; your next step is to be able to accurately communicate to people just what it is you do.

Not with a title, not with a ton of marketing tools but with a simple story. I like to describe it as envisioning the harvest first to determine the seed you will plant. What does your overall brand look like? What impact does it make? How does it make people feel? How does it make people respond?

Branding, this word has been searched over a trillion times on google! It is becoming very common for anyone with a social media account to want to consider becoming a brand.

Whether it is to get free products, to create additional income, or just for the likes, it is the craze of our world today. I truly think we have Reality TV to thank for that. Ever since The Kardashian Family took the stage and dominated the Reality TV world with their blended family drama, luxury lifestyles, merchandising, etc.

It has set a new standard for what it means to build your empire and build your brand!

But whether you are building a personal brand like The Kardashians, Oprah, Will Smith or organizational like Starbucks, Apple, Amazon or Uber there are several things that one should take into consideration before developing a brand. I narrowed it down to these four areas, The M-Factor if you will, they are as follows: *Magnetism, Money Flow, Manpower and Mental Strength.*

Magnetism:

Magnetism is the ability to attract and charm people. Every successful brand has to be appealing, attractive, and mesmerizing. Ask yourself, do people want what I have to offer?

Growing up in Brooklyn, New York in the 80's was such an amazing experience! I can remember when I was just 7 years old, being at our block party with the streets barricaded, water gushing out of the fire hydrant, dance battles and double-dutch contests, it was the best.

I would spend hours with my girlfriends practicing dance moves in preparation for our block parties, it was something serious. I can remember laughing, playing and having the best time when suddenly interrupted by this strong, sultry, captivating voice and catchy beat from the DJ's speakers.

The minute the crowd heard the intro to the music they went berserk! "It's the new girl, Whitney Houston…" It was unforgettable!

Her song, "How Will I Know," was the latest craze! I was hooked, from that day on I was officially a Whitney Houston FANATIC!

I was not the only one obviously, she was the "IT" girl with the "IT" voice. People could not get enough of her. If she wore it, they bought it. If she sang it, they purchased it. We were all hypnotized, mesmerized, magnetized!

Now I know you may be thinking, I am no Whitney Houston! But I want you to embrace this principle and see how it applies to you.

I have come to the realization that fulfilling a need is not enough to secure your brands success, but it is "the desire" for what you offer that does. Do people only need what you have to offer, or do they desire it?

Manpower

Manpower is pretty self-explanatory; it is your ability to attract and/or hire the right team. Every successful brand needs a DREAM TEAM!

As an Entrepreneur, CEO Chick™, Boss, Visionary it is so vital to know your lane. To understand the importance of staffing for your weaknesses.

I find myself often reminding the women of our network of this very thing. Just because you can make the cookies does not mean you know how to run the bakery.

I have lost count of the numerous talented people who are closing shop for this purpose. They are wearing all the hats in their company even though they suck at it.

Consider Apple, where would Steve Wozniak, the inventor of The Apple I Computer be if he did not have a Steve Jobs. Where would Kim Kardashian be without "Momager", Kris Jenner, who trademarked that term by the way.

I want you to ask yourself, who is on your team? Truth be told some entrepreneurs have no clue what they need, or what to ask for.

In this guide we will dive into the various areas required for your brand to thrive, so you can easily assess and identify what you need.

Money Flow

Money Flow is just as important as Manpower and Magnetism. Are you financially prepared to go the long haul!

In the HBO Series, Silicon Valley, the socially awkward, tech savvy programmer turn CEO, Richard Hendricks develops a compression algorithm which takes the Valley by storm.

Several seasons of the show is spent unfolding his journey to seek proper funding for his idea to hit the market. I love this series for the simple fact that it highlights the M-Factor.

It plays out the branding and business process of the characters company, Pied Piper. From logo creation, product development, staffing, sales, partnerships, negotiations, legal contracts, competitors, finances, marketing and more.

Cash flow is often called currency, it moves, it goes up, it comes down. Next to time and relationships it is one of the most important tools needed to build a strong, successful brand.

It is the fuel that takes your business from the runway, to take off, to destination, only to hit the runway yet again. Ask yourself, do you have access to the finances needed to take my brand to its destination?

Do you know how much it will cost to run and expand your business? This and more are the very topics we will discuss in detail as we move further into The Brand To Bucks Guide.

Mental Strength

Have you ever admired the career of a singer, actor or well-known Executive only to wake up one morning to discover the news is reporting they died due to suicide? Amazing people like:

- Robin Williams at 63 years old, famous actor/comedian known for films such as, "World's Greatest Dad" and "Mrs Doubtfire."
- Don Cornelius at 78 years old, host of the famous American "Soul Train."
- Alexander McQueen at 40 years old, famous fashion designer.
- Sawyer Sweeten at 19 years old, famous actor from "Everybody loves Raymond."
- Marilyn Monroe at 36 years old, famous actress and poster child for the beauty industry in her day.
- Lowell Hawthorne at 57 years old, CEO of Golden Krust Caribbean Bakery.
- Titi Branch at 45 years old, Co-Founder of Miss Jessie's Hair Care Products.

The list goes on! In fact, while reviewing the final edit for this book we lost two more amazing souls. Fashion Designer Kate Spade and Celebrity Chef Anthony Bourdain both committed suicide in June of 2018. That is why this M-Factor is so important. *How do you handle stress? Do you take the time to measure your thoughts?* You may be thinking committing suicide is far from you and maybe you are right but that does not exclude you.

Your emotional intelligence and ability to manage stress directly affects your health. It determines our duration and quality of life.

Do you overeat when you are stressed? Do you become violent with others when you are upset? Do you turn to any unhealthy vices to cope with your stress?

I can remember watching rapper and entertainer Clifford Joseph Harris Jr., also known as TI in an episode of TI and Tiny on VH1. During one particular show he was discussing business etiquette with his oldest son.

He made this comment, "Pressure bust pipes, but it also creates diamonds." That stuck with me!

Entrepreneurs can have the money, the dream team, they can be magnetizing, but in the end, their mental and emotional health will determine if they crumble and fold or produce something magical under the pressures of 'success'.

Mental health is a topic I often discuss with my network. I even employed a Mental Health Therapist to teach the members of my network how to handle the stress that comes with running a successful business. Wellness is key, mind, body and spirit!

Well alright Mr. CEO, you ready?! Are you ready CEO Chick? The M-Factor is just the beginning. I really wanted to open this guide with some thought-provoking content.

It is my desire that every entrepreneur takes the time to sit and meditate on these four M's before launching any of their big ideas.

Taking any concept to creation is going to require each of these principles and since knowing is half the battle the good news is these are areas that can be developed.

You may not have everything in place, but I guarantee you this guide will help you get there! So, let's get started!

Your Story

What is your story? Who are you? Why do you do what you do? What problem(s) do you solve?

Your brand's story is what entices customers and your ability to deliver is what makes them your loyal patrons. You may have heard the expression, "storytelling is not dead."

Undoubtedly, this statement holds true in every sense. A key component of your story is your core message. A core message is the angle a business or company takes to target the right publications and the desired audiences. Using the power of storytelling will help you effectively relay your core message.

Did you have that one family member or friend who used to tell you stories about life back in the day? Or the neighborhood grandmother who would tell the best life lessons in soap opera or fairy tale style? Remember how children used to gather around them to feed their curiosity?

Consider your brand in the same way. No, I'm not suggesting that you start spinning tales like a grandmother. However, you must deliver a substantial and informative brand story if you want people to notice you.

The story should be real, descriptive, authentic, and relatable for customers. I want you to think about your overall brand as a book.

Each story in the book is comprised of vibrant, juicy, engaging, descriptive, pieces of information about your brand. Your stories will be the messaging that your marketing content will be made from.

I recently tasked one of our CEO Chick Members to a simple challenge. I shared with her the importance of leading with a story when she met potential clients versus her title.

Financial Advisor, Sirnollia was having a hard time getting leads at networking events. I told her to be more creative and unassuming in her conversations, to lead with a story that briefly describes the problem she solves.

This chapter describes in detail the advice I gave her. Long story short she followed my guidance and was surprised at the results. Where she would normally have zero leads, she landed 5 at the networking event she frequents.

Tell a story! Work your magic, create something tantalizing and captivating.

Power of Authentic Storytelling

Why is authentic storytelling so important for you and your business?

It connects brands and people in a personal manner rather than relying on traditional promotional methods. The advent of the internet and a global culture offers many benefits such as fast connectivity with people worldwide, access to information with the click of your finger, and easily transferable data.

While the digital age offers a myriad of benefits, it has taken away something deep inside us: our real essence. This does not necessarily mean people are fake, but we often crave a more natural, "in the flesh" type of connection.

The more mechanized and industrialized we become, the more we crave nature and personal connection. The more our culture clings to tablets, cell phones, or any other devices the more we desire the human touch. This is where your story comes in.

There are many other brands and businesses out there, so why would customers choose you over them? Develop a rapport with customers and they'll gravitate to you.

Let's take a B2B BREAK right here.

This is where I want you to take a minute to reflect on the topic in discussion and write down your thoughts. I want you to consider where you are regarding story selling. Take a moment and answer the following questions:

Who is your ideal audience?

_____
_____
_____
_____

Have you been sharing your authentic story with your core audience? Briefly write down the parts of your story you share with your audience.

_____
_____
_____
_____

What portions of your story can your ideal audience relate or connect to?

_____
_____
_____
_____

Authentic storytelling is important if you want to connect with your customers on a more personal and profound level. People not only crave a premium product, but a personal connection as well. Regardless of how useful your products and services are, the inability to connect with customers will hinder your business.

Why Does Authentic Storytelling Work?

- It helps distinguish you from the competition and elevate your status in the market
- It establishes you as an influential entity while building a reliable and trustworthy reputation
- It strengthens your products and services and maintains the focus of your vision
- It serves as the face of your business
- It links you and your customers by conveying your products' benefits
- It engraves you in the minds of your customers and earns their loyalty
- It creates an everlasting bond between you and your customers

'People Trust People': Build Trust With Your Customers

Trust building is a time-consuming task that requires a lot of hard work and effort from businesses. Businesses spend thousands of dollars building their relationships with clients and customers because they know that trustworthiness is essential to leaving a lasting impression. There are numerous ways to earn your customers' trust.

Be Approachable

Businesses that are open and easily accessible to customers are considered more reliable than those hiding behind multiple layers of secrecy. The best way to ensure your customers can reach you easily is by providing complete details. Include your address, phone numbers, fax number, email address and availability.

Train your customer service staff to interact with customers in an effective and helpful manner to address all their concerns. The more open you are with customers, the more they will trust you.

Offer Great Services

There is another way to gain the trust of customers and clients. If you want people to trust you and remain loyal, you have to offer great services and products at all levels.

To make sure you are offering something invaluable and beneficial to your clients, listen to their needs, interact with them, encourage them to give feedback, and tailor your services and products accordingly.

Connect with your audience through social media and inform them of the improvements you have made based on their feedback.

Consistency

Consistency is the key to creating long-lasting relationships with your customers and employees. If you want to give a memorable experience to customers, then you have to treat your employees well. This will ensure that your employees are ready to share your vision and willing to work with you.

Inform employees about your expectations and tell customers what they can expect from you. Once you have declared these expectations, live up to them consistently. People take notice of your actions, so you are mistaken if you believe you can earn loyalty solely by offering good services.

Give A Personal Touch

Do you want to create a deeper and meaningful relationship with your customers?

Connect with them personally on a deeper level. People like it when their favorite businesses or brands show an interest in their personal lives. To create a personal relationship, reemphasize the importance of friendliness to your customer support staff and ensure they interact with customers via social media.

Another way to build connections beyond business is by sharing stories about your personal life and the work environment.

Everyone loves the underdog, the tragedy to triumph, rags to riches story. Think of times in your life where the odds were against you and you lost it all, but you got it back!

I meet people with incredible stories like this all the time, but they don't want to share it. They prefer the "I got it all together" approach but that does not go very far. People are dealing with daily resistances to their dreams, they are constantly fighting to accomplish their goals.

They are looking for people that can relate to them, that have solutions to the problems they are facing. Sharing your story helps your ideal client find you. *The truth is people buy the 'who' before they buy the 'what'!* I teach my clients how to leverage their losses. How can your most painful experiences pay you back? By sharing your story!

Three-Part Storytelling Module

You may be reading this and saying to yourself, "I have a hard time talking to people period, let alone telling them a story about my life."

I totally get it! The good thing about telling your story is it is no different from learning how to read one. It's one thing to share a story; it is an entirely different experience to transform the lives of others through compelling authentic storytelling.

I have listed three components of storytelling I want you to begin to practice. Once you master these three, you will naturally begin to use it in conversations in the grocery store, networking events, or speaking on platforms.

You will find your conversions will increase as well as your level of influence. This will build anticipation and engage your ideal customers.

They will want to hear your story and learn more about you and your business. I often remind my clients that people buy the 'who' before they buy the 'what'. In other words, they want to know who you are, and what you have to offer before they consider handing over their money. So, let's take a look.

1st Part: State the Problem

Before offering a solution, you have to consider the problem you hope to address through your products or services. Identify the problem and frame your story around it.

2nd Part: How Will You Solve It?

After identifying the problem and relaying it to your customers, describe how you will solve the problem. Be pragmatic and come up with solutions your audience can connect with.

3rd Part: Connecting The Story To Your Customers

Ensure the story resonates with your customers and it relates to their problems. As a result, customers will personally connect with you because they will feel reassured.

Let's take a B2B BREAK right here.

This is where we take a minute to reflect on the topic in discussion and write down our thoughts. I want you to consider where you are regarding story selling. Take a moment and answer the following questions:

State a problem you can solve:

_____
_____
_____
_____

List how you will solve this problem:

_____
_____
_____
_____

Connect the story to your customer, list the outcome your client experienced because of your product or service:

_____
_____
_____
_____

Get Others To Tell Your Story

Storytelling is like a campaign; its success is determined by the way people conceive it and follow it. If presented effectively, storytelling sets you apart from others in business. Successful businesses not only have great stories, but they also have great storytelling techniques that inspire followers to share them.

When it comes to marketing, many people try to do everything on their own and become stressed. Marketing is an essential component of your business. It is how you communicate the essence of your business to the public, so people will become interested and invested in your business. As more and more people become interested in your business, they will most likely spread the word about your business. Wouldn't it be easier if customers reduced your workload by sharing your story with others?

How Does Storytelling Motivate Your Fans To Share Your Story?

This is a great marketing tactic that connects your brand with customers, fosters loyalty, and encourages customers to "spread the word" for you.

According to Uri Hasson, a researcher at Princeton, storytelling influences brain activity by indulging listeners' emotional side of the brain, and evoking empathy by connecting them with the business' chronicle.

An actionable story consists of four parts:
- **Goal:** A great story starts with a *goal*. Why do you want to tell the story, and what will you tell in it?
- **Grab Attention:** It *grabs attention* with a powerful opening and compelling story line.
- **Engage:** It *engages* customers by maintaining their focus.
- **Enable Action:** Finally, it *enables action* by inciting them to carry out your desired action.

➤ Ways To Motivate Others To Tell Your Story

If you want your audience to share your story, then you must motivate them and provide incentives for taking action. Due to the steadily increasing number of marketing ads, people have short attention spans regarding brands. There's so much information to process they quickly forget about particular brands.

In this scenario, it becomes even more challenging to retain customers and cause them to act as your advocates, however, it's not impossible. There are numerous ways to motivate your audience to share your story with others.

Be Specific With What You Offer

Before telling a story, you should determine what you will offer clients. This is important because it will form the basis of your story and motivate your audience. Be as detailed as possible when describing what you offer. Your audience needs to know what they are receiving to spread information to others.

Listen To Your Ideal Clients And Customers

You want to cater to your customers' needs, right? How will you do this if you don't know their requirements? To solve this dilemma, it's necessary to listen to your customers and learn about their diverse needs.

Once you have designed your services and products based on customers' needs, they will start sharing your story and services with other people. Now take a moment to think of a product you would like to sell.

Let's take a B2B BREAK right here.

What's one product and/or service you want to create within 90 days based on the problem you know how to solve?

_____
_____
_____
_____
_____

Be Different From Your Competitors

I absolutely love it when a new company shows up in a "saturated" space and wins! Based on your assessment of your product or services you may get discouraged if you see a ton of companies doing the same thing.

You may talk yourself out of launching or going forward because the market is saturated but in fact this may be a reason why you should move forward. I think about companies like Wahlburgers or Five Guys that entered the Hamburger space and are thriving! *Don't get discouraged but get a plan!*

Why should customers choose you over your competitors? What makes you different? How do you add or create value to them?

Your customers need to know everything about your business. Present yourself as a solution to their problems by informing them of the beneficial features of your services and products.

Promote your own products, but don't devalue your competitors because it will backfire. Instead, explain how your business meets their requirements.

Be Consistent! Stay On Their Mind

For customers to remember you, you must constantly remind them about your business. In today's corporate world, it's easier to lose clients than gain them. Therefore, make sure to tell your story whenever you have the chance. Instead of repeating the same facts, be innovative and creative.

Talk about the progression of your business, your experiences, people behind the scenes, and other insightful information. This way you will sound less promotional and more conversational.

Show That You Value Customers

Take feedback from your customers and communicate with them directly. You can ask for their feedback in multiple ways. One option is to send a survey via email that asks for their input regarding services and products. Analyze the data and make any necessary improvements to your business operations. Your customers will feel appreciated and share your story.

Benefits of Social Media

Social media benefits businesses in countless ways. It's no longer solely used for socializing with friends and family. Prevailing trends have made social media a necessity for businesses to communicate and interact with customers and potential clients.

There are multiple social platforms and that offer various benefits. One benefit is that social media enables you to convey your business and brand story in an effective and far-reaching manner. Besides using it as a powerful storytelling tool, social media planning should be an essential part of your overall marketing and business strategy.

While planning a social media campaign, especially the one focused on your story, you should consider and answer the following questions:
- What is your story about?
- What do you want to tell through your story?
- Have you chosen the right medium(s) for the task?
- Who is your target market?
- Is your story resonating with them?
- Is it evoking any strong emotions in your audience?
- Is it enough to connect your audience with your business?
- Will it make the audience take the desired action you intended?
- Will it cause them to share it?
- Will it gain their loyalty?

This may seem like a lot of work, but it's necessary to have a clear picture of your social media campaign. Once you have thoroughly planned your strategy, it will be much easier to convey your message and share your story with potential customers and audiences. Even after you have detailed your strategy, you still need to navigate through a plethora of social media platforms. Since there are so many different platforms, it can be a somewhat confusing ordeal.

A Word of Caution

Every social media platform is different and all of them are not geared towards meeting your goals. Decide what you want to achieve and choose the right medium for you.

Benefits of Social Media Platforms

What are the benefits of different social media platforms and how can they help convey your exclusive brand story?

Each social media platform functions differently, so you need to have a variety of strategies to fully and effectively utilize them. Seeing it as one size does not fit all, the same approach is not suitable for every platform. Determine the most appropriate ways to interact with your audience.

The following six platforms will help you promote your business and its ideals to customers in an influential way:

Facebook will connect you with customers and potential clients and create new opportunities. Set up a business page for your company and invite employees and associates to initiate the conversation. Since this platform is more informal and casual, try to keep the conversations light-hearted and engaging. Your customers will love talking to you and getting to know you better. They can also write reviews on your business, view your content and shop your merchandise.

Instagram/ Pinterest is what I call an online catalog, its image driven. Do not underestimate its influence and ability to elevate your customer interactions. If you have "shareworthy" photos or 60 second videos post them to take full advantage of this platform. Post images of your products, events your company has hosted and attended, team gatherings, people at work, and much more. Statistics show users of these platforms are customers looking to buy. Use your feed to tell your story and paint a picture of your brand experience.

Twitter is your number one communicative tool. Facebook and Google+ are influential interactive tools, but if you want to maintain constant contact with your connections, then Twitter is your best option. Tweets are generally short (maximum 140 characters) and you should aim for 8 to 10 tweets a day. However, you can be as communicative and 'tweetable' as you want. The more tweets, the better.

LinkedIn is a more professional platform and is primarily used for various business purposes. This is a great way to keep all of your business connections on a single platform and connect with them. It is also a great place to make your business a trustworthy entity while marketing your content simultaneously. You can share your business' story on your professional page by discussing your background, goals, and major achievements. Join LinkedIn Groups, interact with other businesses in the Questions Section, and fortify your presence by asking clients and loyal customers to write recommendations on your page.

Google+ functions similarly to Facebook and facilitates your connections with followers. You can share things such as photos, videos, visual content, articles, and blogs within your circle. Google+ also gives you the ability to make separate and exclusive Google+ Circles to share content with them. This also means that you can restrict other connections from seeing the content.

While the platforms may not be equally viable for every business, there are numerous ways to make them work for you. One of the best things about these social platforms is that you can utilize them for storytelling purposes regardless of their specific functions.

Your business story is a coveted asset. People connect with businesses better when they cater to their visual needs. They will be stimulated and frequently replay your story in their minds. In any case, you need to gain the trust and loyalty of customers if you want them to share your story with their inner circle.

Let's take a B2B BREAK right here.

Now that you have practice writing your own story using the 3-part method, I want you to take some time to write short posts you can use on social media to target your audience. Implement the previously mentioned components to create an engaging story that markets your brand.

When I share my struggles and success in conjunction with an image or video it tends to increase my online engagements.

I will often pull out a key piece of information or principle I learned in my ongoing journey.

The goal is to leave people inspired, educated and wanting more.

Brand To Bucks

Your Style

Gone are the days of thinking, "I am a businessperson, so why do I need to pay attention to my style and image? After all, people are here to do business with me, not focus on my attire!"

If this is your mentality, then you are in for a surprise. People often consider the way you dress and carry yourself when deciding whether they want to work with you. The good news is, you are not the only person who thinks this way. Many business people overlook this theory because they belong to many organizations where perhaps they were not the face of the brand, or they were not responsible for pitching their ideas to potential investors. When you move from being the employee to the CEO, the rules change.

Lets' be upfront and honest here. No one, at first glance, will choose to hire the over-weight personal trainer when looking for someone to help them with their weight loss goals. They would not walk into a salon for the first time and select the stylist with the worst hair to perform their service.

Who walks into a tattoo parlor and says, "give me the clean-cut tattoo artist without a tattoo in site!" People want to do business with people that have been successful in the areas that they too desire to experience wins.

Customers, especially now, know exactly what they want! They have done the research, they have checked out your website, visited your social media pages, read online reviews.

The internet is full of these studious, professional consumers, I call them the pro-sumers. Remember the good ole' statement still stands true today, "first impressions create a lasting impression," you must dress to impress!

When I first began working at a salon that catered to mainly Caucasian clients, I wore my hair in an afro and wrapped it up like Erika Badu (Afrocentric Music Artist). I was in this bead and incense phase in my life.

I can remember the day when our District Manager came by, as they often did, to observe the salons and she asked to speak to me in the office. This was before my management days with this salon chain, but she talked to me about my appearance. She told me my image could give off the wrong impression to the clients and recommended some changes that could increase my productivity. Let me just go ahead and tell you, I was flat out offended!

How dare she tell me to change my look! I left that office in a silent rage, finished my shift and went home. I was done with that place; they just want to change me I thought!

Then about 48 hours later it hit me. Why would a white male think this black girl with her head wrapped like a beautiful African Goddess know anything about cutting my hair?

What if the roles were reversed? Would I be confident in thinking he could do my hair? It was not that I was being racially profiled per say, or I would not be working there at all. She wanted to simply give me wisdom that could help me gain the trust of potential clients.

This advice taught me something about the power of appearance. It is the same reason hard criminals wear a suit in court or why we go out of our way to make a lasting impression on a first date.

The way you dress, walk, talk communicates to people who you are, it's an expression of your personality.

Your persona can draw or distract someone from wanting to get to know more about you. For instance, suppose you attend a party. What kind of woman would you choose to spend your evening with?

Someone who lacks refinement and manners, or a woman who carries herself elegantly? The same goes for businessmen too. What type of man would you choose? A man with a timid demeanor or someone who is suave and confident? Weigh your options and make the logical choices. If you desire successful and long-lasting business partnerships, then you should treat your business contacts as life partners in a meaningful relationship.

It might sound strange, but have you ever noticed how personal relationships and business relationships have a lot in common? Both are precious to you and require a lot of work to maintain them. Still thinking it over? Let's look at how a relationship starts:

- You search for the most suitable partner
- Assess your compatibility and rapport
- Make a vow of loyalty to each other
- Strive to improve the relationship with each passing day

Now consider your business partnerships or connections. Don't you repeat the same steps while establishing a corporate relationship?

Yes, you do. You also must face similar consequences if you break those vows in either case. So, the very first step in determining how to carry yourself is to view your business connections as personal relationships. When you go on a date, you want to look presentable. How many of you would go on a date in a raggedy shirt and crumpled jeans?

The answer should be, 'no one'. A business meeting is just as important, and you should have your wardrobe filled with professional and stylish clothes.

Personal Style

Every individual is different with a unique personality and style. Just because you are in the business world, it does not mean you should relinquish your personality. Amidst your business obligations, you have to maintain your individuality.

You must be careful and considerate when revamping your wardrobe. This rule applies to both genders in business. Your style also ties into your business and if it does not, then you step back and re-evaluate.

To define your personal style, have some staple pieces at your disposal. You might think this is expensive, but it is not. If you choose the right kind of clothes and know how to creatively revitalize them, then you can dazzle people with just a few articles of clothing.

What are the essentials for men and women in business? Read on.

Must Have Staple Pieces for Men

Fashion is always changing and keeping up with trends can be daunting. To ensure that you are stylish, maintain the following staple pieces for a man's wardrobe. These pieces should be enough and will not require a large budget. Moreover, once you have created your wardrobe, you will not have to follow fashion trends, unless, of course, you really want to.

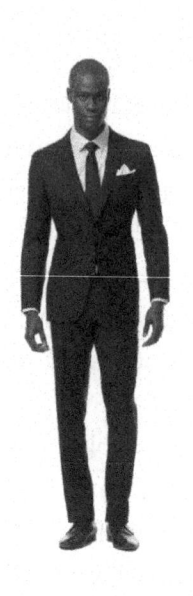

A Perfectly Tailored Black Suit

All men, even if they are not involved in business, should have one perfectly tailored black or grey suit.

Why black or grey? Both colors are versatile, and you will not have to worry whether they are in fashion or not. They are always in fashion and suitable for every occasion.

A bonus is that these suits are extremely durable and can be worn for years with proper care.

A Crisp White Shirt

This is the most essential article of your wardrobe. A white shirt is as versatile as your black or grey suit because it looks professional and can be worn for various occasions.

To have a perfect and professional look, the shirt should be perfectly tailored for your body type and build. A loose or overly fitted shirt will have the opposite effect. To add some variety, you can also wear crisp shirts in other colors like blue, indigo and the classic black.

Denim Jeans In A Darker Tone

These are perfect for people uncomfortable with wearing clothes that are deemed too trendy or fashionable. Skinny jeans have been in fashion for quite some time, but if you want a timeless look, have a pair of straight cut jeans in your wardrobe. You can pair it with a polo or a buttoned shirt and coat for both a professional or casual look.

A Cashmere Sweater

Cashmere is no longer a feminine thing; it can give you the classic masculine look and is perfect for several occasions.

Going to the office? You can wear it in colder months. Even during the holidays, it is the perfect piece. When buying one, choose solid and darker colors like black, navy blue, brown or grey. Always make sure to read the washing instructions carefully.

A Navy-Blue Blazer

A navy-blue blazer is ideal even if you do not already have a tailored suit. It is classic and versatile. This color complements all your professional and casual attire. You can wear it in a meeting or when you are hanging out with your friends.

As with any other jacket, it needs to be tailored properly to have the desired professional look and effect. If it's too big or small, it will ruin your look. Match it with your casual jeans or professional pants to have various looks.

A Good Watch

We love watches, and the reason is simple; they exude style and personality. That is why you need to have one that accentuates your professional self. You can choose from an array of collections including leather or metal bands. As far as colors are concerned, consider darker shades like black, brown, and navy blue for leather straps and gold or silver for metallic bands.

You do not need to spend a lot of money; all you need is a clean watch with a professional look.

A Pair Of Professional Oxfords

A pair of oxfords is a necessity in your wardrobe. If you work in an office that follows a more formal dress code, then a pair of professional oxfords is your best choice.

If you have some flexibility, then you can opt for a pair of neutral loafers. It is best to choose them in black or brown since both colors are universal. You can easily pair them with your, less formal, khakis or with a full professional suit.

Must Have Staple Pieces For Women

Like men, women also need to follow a professional dress code at work. Unlike men, they do have a little more flexibility, but there are some pieces that should form the foundation of their wardrobe.

Regardless of age, body shape, or height, the seven following pieces should be included in every woman's wardrobe:

A Pencil Skirt

If you only want one skirt, then it should be the pencil skirt. It is classy, elegant, and suitable for every occasion. It goes well with any body shape and equally complements blouses, jackets and sweaters.

Pencil skirts are part of classic business and office attire for women as its knee length makes it all-purpose. Choose one that is perfect for your body shape and will not loosen throughout the day.

A Trench Coat

This is also great for every occasion because it will never go out of fashion and can be worn with a pair of jeans or professional pants.

It is classic, flattering, functional, and offers great waist detail. Thanks to its at waist tie option, it goes well with everybody type and can be worn for work or a casual meeting. When choosing one, go for medium lapels, and a double-breasted bodice with a tie at the waist.

A Tailored Suit

Yes, you read it correctly. Tailored suits are as equally important for women as they are for men. They are professional and give the impression that you mean business. To have the essentially perfect and professional look, ensure that it's tailored appropriately, according to your body shape and type.

We stress proper fitting because a poorly fitted suit will not have the required effect. Choose classic colors like black, dark grey, or navy blue.

Classic Black Pumps

There is nothing wrong with open toe sandals, flats, or loafers but when it comes to making an impression, you cannot go wrong with black pumps.

They are classic, and you can wear them with almost anything, jeans, skirts, suits, you name it. For many, shoes can be a lifetime or long-lasting investment, and black pumps are a prime example. Choose a closed, almond-shaped toe in matte leather that will last throughout the seasons.

A Blue Blazer

Again, not only meant for men. It is also very important for women. A blue blazer is versatile and offers a wider range of usage and looks. Women need to have at least a pair of blue blazers in their wardrobe. They are great for complementing your trendiest clothes and will give them more personality. When choosing a blue blazer, select one that is at hip length because it will accentuate legs and waists equally.

A White Buttoned Shirt Or A White Blouse

A white buttoned up shirt or a classic white blouse is best for every occasion and a great professional item in your wardrobe. It matches well with casual jeans and a blazer, professional pants, or with suits and skirts. As always, it should be well-fitted. They are available in different materials like cotton and chiffon and are ideal for professional and causal meetings.

A Little Black Dress

Here comes the star of the evening, the little black dress (LBD). What makes the little black dress so trendy and classic? Its simplicity and ease of usage of course. Because it is so simple with a minimal design, it can be worn in business meetings, work, weddings, and even casual gatherings with friends or family.

The ideal length for a black dress is up to the knees or a bit shorter. Due to its minimal design, you can mix and match it with shoes and accessories to give it a personal touch.

Let's take a B2B BREAK right here.

Now that you understand personal styles for business, jot down some clothing pieces that are in your wardrobe. Next, take the time to answer the questions below. Create your own personal style using the pieces listed in this chapter.

What items do you currently have in your wardrobe from the above list? Write them below.

_____

_____

_____

_____

_____

What are the items from this chapter that you will need to add to your wardrobe?

_____

_____

_____

_____

_____

Fashion Sense

Do you know what is greater than being fashionable? There is nothing like an individual that is not just cute but cute with content!

That is right, this is what I call Fashion Sense. You may have noticed that many highly successful people are avid readers. They spend much of their time reading inspirational and useful books.

I am a firm believer that wealth is on the other side of what you do not know. The knowledge you need for your next level of greatness is in a book. To have substance you must remain a student. Continuing to learn, read, travel, and absorb information makes for great conversation when networking, or even when developing speaking points for larger audiences.

To keep you inspired, I have compiled a list of the top 10 books that are on the shelves of successful CEOs and people. These books are based on the everyday things in life that impact our behavior and success factors.

The list includes:
- The Power Of Positive Thinking—Norman Vincent Peale
- The Checklist Manifesto—Atul Gawande
- Long Walk To Freedom – Nelson Mandela
- The Ascent Of Money—Niall Ferguson
- Tribal Leadership—Dave Logan
- Built To Last—Jim Collins
- The 7 Habits Of Highly Effective People—Stephen Covey
- How To Win Friends And Influence People—Dale Carnegie
- Think And Grow Rich—Napoleon Hill
- As A Man Thinketh – James Allen

The Power Of Positive Thinking

This book is written by Norman Vincent Peale and is an international bestseller. We all want to have a successful and fulfilling life, but many of us do not know what it takes to achieve and live this dream.

This book is powerful and reflective of a general perspective on life. It is nothing short of a gold mine for people struggling to be more successful. If you are one of these people, grab your edition now! It can be equally beneficial for others as well.

The Checklist Manifesto

Written by Atul Gawande, the book is about the balance crisis. Having more work to do and not enough time to manage it all. People have become busier and have more tasks to complete, which leaves them short on time and often stressed and frustrated.

The writer attempts to address the situation with the power of making checklists. It has been said on a number of occasions that planning is the key to success and better performance. Checklists help keep you on track and this book sheds light on this aspect.

Long Walk To Freedom

Nelson Mandela is one of the greatest activists of all time and his autobiography details his journey to becoming an eminent social figure. Everyone knows about Nelson Mandela's life and purpose. His life was full of hardships and severe conditions and the book reveals those times. It chronicles political strife, conflicts, struggles, hope and the success that occurred in Mandela's life. If you look closely, our lives are also filled with adversity, which is why the book has earned a place on our list.

The Ascent Of Money

The book is written by Niall Ferguson and documents the origins of money, how it works, and what are the key factors to earn it. This book is perfect for people who are interested in financial matters and learning ways to manage them.

It is also useful for aspiring businesspeople and entrepreneurs because it will teach you about important money matters that will help you manage financial affairs in business.

Tribal Leadership

Written by Dave Logan, the book is an incredible account of how connection and interaction contribute to the success of businesses and brands. People yearn for connections and gain an affinity for brands they can identify with personally. The writer has examined facts that make connecting with people productive. He also explores reasons why this is successful in the corporate world.

Built To Last

The book is written by Jim Collins and assesses key factors that make some businesses successful while others are mediocre or struggling. We all know that it requires special skills and persistence to be successful, great, and unforgettable, but how many of us really understand those skills or factors? Unfortunately, only a few people know this information. If you want to learn more, grab your copy.

The 7 Habits Of Highly Effective People

Written by Stephen R. Covey, no list of inspirational books is complete without this one. If you have read the book, then it is obvious why it is so influential. The book records the top seven qualities and habits of effective and influential people. These are all components that contributed to their effectiveness and can be developed by anyone.

While reading the book, you will also notice that many people lack these habits. This differentiates us from people who have developed them. Add this book to your collection if you want to have a pragmatic way of developing habits for success.

How To Win Friends And Influence People

The book is written by Dale Carnegie and at the time of its composition, mixing of professional and personal relationships was considered taboo. People did not want these relationships to merge and they tried to keep them in separate categories.

Carnegie challenged the status quo and subsequently, blending professional and personal relationships became an absolute business necessity. The writer talks about the compatibility of personal and professional relationships and the reasons why they should be kept together for your success. If you are still skeptical, I suggest you read this book.

Think And Grow Rich

Written by Napoleon Hill, the book is based on the true experiences of millionaires, their journey to success, and factors that contributed to it. Hill interviewed forty millionaires and stated that their journeys went from nothing to greatness.

The book challenges the common belief that success and wealth are the outcomes of greed and a healthy dash of luck. It is a must read for entrepreneurs and business students because it encapsulates proven tactics of successful people.

As A Man Thinketh

A man is the product of the thoughts he holds. This book sheds further light on that statement. In a society that believes actions are key factors to success, James Allen broke away from mainstream logic. He argued that thoughts design and mold a personality, not actions.

The book talks about how and why dreamers and thinkers are the ones who can change the world. Allen explained the process by which how an individual think influences habits, personality, and actions.

Having a carefully designed wardrobe and a collection of books is essential for men and women. If you still doubt my claim, then think of it this way: every person you meet does not know anything about you, your business, your skills, or your reputation. He or she knows absolutely nothing about you, so how do they decide whether they want to have a business relationship with you?

The answer is simple: the way you carry yourself. Aloof people are not considered attractive for any relationship. People who know how to carry themselves will appeal to everyone.

It is commonly known a person is judged by the company they keep. Add extra luster to your style and keep useful books at your disposal. Remember you want *style and substance*!

Let's take a B2B BREAK right here.

Write a list of books that have personally influenced you. Then write some topics you would like to read about and research some books to add to your collection to expand your knowledge.

Create a list of topics and books you would like to read for personal development. Set a date to complete the books of your choice.

_____

_____
_____
_____
_____
_____
_____
_____
_____
_____
_____
_____
_____
_____
_____
_____
_____
_____
_____
_____
_____

Your Skills

Nothing hurts a business more than being unable to deliver on their brand promise. Unfortunately, the anxiety and pressure caused by social media or a focus on our competitors, can make even the most experienced entrepreneur put out an idea that has not been properly vetted.

"Coming soon!" "Pre-order now!" "Stay tuned!" All too often are the words of premature ads that build people up only to let them down because there was not a plan in place.

Some years ago, I met a woman, let's call her Lindsey, she was gorgeous, smart, business savvy and always had something great going on.

As time progressed and I got to know her more I diagnosed her with what I call, the **"launch lust"** syndrome. Every month she had a different idea "launching"! They were totally unrelated to one another, she marketed them all on the same social media platform with her headshot as the face of her latest big idea. Lindsey didn't stick to anything; she was always in the process of shutting something down and setting something up.

Every idea had an amazing hashtag but regardless of the "#buildinganempire" message, we were left as feeling "#confused".

It was draining just witnessing her go thru this grueling process. Were there any long-term goals attached to each concept? Was there a team in place with the proper training and tools to maintain every idea she had?

Maybe you are suffering from a bit of ***"launch lust"*** syndrome. Itching at every chance to showcase a new idea, a fresh concept, the next hot thing on your agenda! Lets' take a lesson out the pages of Lindsey's brand book and not repeat this unsavory behavior.

What we produce is more important that what we post. In other words, we should not market what we do not have the ability to manage.

Understanding your limitations and knowing your strengths will allow you to determine what you can and cannot deliver!

Under promise and over deliver. Do you need some "special" skills to succeed in your business? No and yes.

No because successful businesspeople all have some common traits that make them stand out from the crowd. And yes because, as every business possesses its own Brand DNA, it is different, so is the unique skill set to run it properly and successfully.

In either case, no one can claim to possess all the required skills or that they know everything. Individuals or organizations who think like this are often left behind and forgotten. They fail to pay attention to the latest trends and don't learn about their customer's current needs. Therefore, people stop considering them an expert or a knowledgeable business leader.

It is a universal fact that people who continually learn new skills are successful and tend to stay in business for a long time. Before venturing on the path of learning new skills, it is advisable to make a list of your existing skills and see if they're compatible with the skills you need for business.

Regarding businesses, the most successful ones are connected and built to support each other. The same goes for new skills; the most beneficial ones work perfectly with your existing skills.

After you have made the list, it is now time to determine what makes your skills unique from others in the market. It is important because if you want to break into a successful business, you have to make a unique offer. Otherwise, why would someone listen to you?

If you want people to listen to you, give them some concrete reasons.

Let's take a B2B BREAK right here.

While considering your list of skills, answer the following questions:

What are your current skill sets?

_____
_____
_____
_____

What makes your skills different from your competitors?

_____
_____
_____
_____

Have you mastered your skills?

_____
_____
_____
_____

What measures are you taking to keep your skills sharp?

_____

_____

_____

_____

_____

Skillsets Of The Successful

What Skills Do You Require To Be Successful In Your Job And Business?

They say hard work beats talent but what's even better is hard work and talent. While there are numerous skills that can help you succeed in your job and business, there are some that can be considered staple skills. Principles, laws, and golden rules that will allow you to thrive in business.

Adaptability

Adapting is a part of a successful life. If you do not want to be left behind, then adaptability is your only and foremost choice.

Many businesses make the mistake of trying to stick to their old ways and fail to adapt or, to evolve to the needs of their customers. As a result, they are forgotten and left behind. Companies like Block Buster, My Space, and Kmart to name a few.

Nothing stays the same forever. Change is essential in life and your business. As per the research by CCL (Center for Creative Leadership), adaptability is the number one factor in the success of North American Managers.

What Are The Key Factors Of Adaptability?

Instead of following the mainstream, find new ways of doing old things and search for ways to work in a better manner. Creativity is a key to innovating existing systems and processes. It should be harnessed by your company and among your teammates.

Having a backup plan is the best way to cope up with any unexpected situations. Do not just rely on a single plan or strategy. Have a plan B and C ready in case your usual plan does not work. Planning also saves time and effort.

You cannot adapt to change successfully and promptly if you do not know what is going on around you. Be curious and question everything. If you are an owner, instill the same curiosity in your company and teammates. Learn about the latest happenings, trends, and news, especially related to your industry and plan.

When the environment, people, expectations, and most importantly, your consumer's needs change, it is better to accept it.

Many businesses mistakenly resist change and lose their clients. Instead, find ways to be a part of it. Make use of your contacts and social media to meet new people and connect with them on a professional and personal level.

Communicate Like A Pro

Communication is key to better relationships and connections. Whether in professional or personal life, if you cannot communicate effectively, people will not know about your views. Regrettably, they may also no longer be interested in knowing anything about you. People who know how to communicate in an effective manner are more successful in their jobs and businesses. How exactly can you master the art of communication?

What Are The Key Factors Of Professional And Effective Communication?

Before speaking or discussing anything, it is better that you know what you are talking about. Many people get confused and puzzle listeners because they muddle their conversation. Plan your thoughts and make mental points of how to start, proceed, and end your conversation.

Avoid talking about trivial things or topics that are unrelated to your business. Another important thing is to not use clichés in your conversation. People want to hear the truth in plain English.

Do not use long sentences and statements. We all love to read, but how many times have you come across an article with long sentences and continued reading without getting bored? Longer sentences lose their meaning and the listener will lose the essence of the whole conversation due to length. Your best bet is to keep sentences short and your conversation concise.

Do not be a fake communicator. People can see straight through you and instantly recognize that you are insincere. The major consequence is that they will never be interested in talking to you again. Everyone has a personality that makes them different from others, and yes, we all possess that unique personality. Let that personality come out and speak. You seem more natural and people will be drawn to you.

Network Like A Pro

Networking is an important aspect of every business;
- How will you find your potential clients?
- How will you market your products and services in a much more effective manner?
- How will you keep updated with the latest happenings of the business world?

The answers to all these questions come from networking with the right group of people and building strong and meaningful relationships. As you require skills to communicate effectively, you also require skills to network effectively as a professional.

What Are The Key Factors Of Professional And Effective Networking?

Plan your networking process beforehand to avoid any possible mishaps. Before going to a conference, identify what type of conference it is and the people who are attending.

A good method is to check the guest list on the website and research them. After finding the closest ones to your market and business niche, select any three that you will communicate with. Choose three more that you will casually converse with during the conference.

After arriving at the conference, scan the room and find the groups you will interact and converse with. Here your observation skills will be put to the test because you have to make the decision solely on the body language of group members. Do they look open to engaging in conversations? If so, you can proceed.

Once you have found your 'ideal' group, do not wait too long; just go ahead and talk to them. The longer you wait, it will be harder for you to join them and engage. Still unsure of how to start? Just approach them and ask whether you can join the conversation.

After you have joined the group, get to know them better. Listen to the way they talk, the things they talk about, and internalize common interests amongst the group. You will converse and network better if you know the people you are talking to. This way you will build a relationship with them. Also, do not forget to add them to your social networks later that evening. The sooner the better.

Invest in the people you meet. Before asking for anything, identify ways to benefit them without expecting anything in return. The best way to do this is by introducing the person you are speaking with to someone else before you shift to another group.

When networking you must be aware of your energy, your body language and confidence level. People are often shocked to find out I am a true introvert. Being an introvert does not mean you have poor people skills, but it simply means it requires intentionality. Here are three attributes I always keep in mind when networking:

Be Aggressive

Being aggressive means pursuing motives and goals with a burning, relentless desire. Now this does not mean you should start throwing temper tantrums or become difficult to work with but be confident, assertive, firm, and kind. I have a saying, 'you don't have to be mean, you just have to mean what you say.'

Successful people do not have a laid-back attitude. They know that this mentality can cost them dearly. Therefore, they stay in "aggressively active" mode. They also know what they want out of life and pursue it fully charged. Until they achieve their goal, they maintain this mindset.

When networking, make eye contact, have a firm handshake, smile, compliment people, ask questions, and have fun!

Never Be Complacent

How will you achieve great things when you are satisfied with good things? People who are content with small things and achievements never have the taste of greatness. It is not because they cannot be great but simply because they are satisfied with mediocrity.

Remarkably successful and great people are always hungry; they are hungry for greatness, they are hungry for change, and they are hungry for an everlasting identity.

Their hunger keeps them going, even when everyone else has stopped. They are never satisfied. This constant unrest keeps them on their heels and enables them to achieve new things.

Do not be afraid to discuss new things you are learning in your entrepreneurial journey while networking. Be open to the input of others, allow people to shine in the conversation. It is okay to be the student in one part of the dialogue and the teacher in the next.

Be Persistent

Persistence is the key to success. No matter how great your ideal business is, if you do not have the courage to continue through thick and thin, you will not be successful.

Many people start their journey with great enthusiasm, but very few keep going even when the situation is bleak. These are the people that succeed in making prominent and unique marks in business.

What Are The Key Attributes Of Persistent People?

Persistent people *do not work without a plan*. They have a vision and goal. In addition, they believe they have a higher purpose in life beyond making a living. They are dreamers who constantly move towards their goal and work tirelessly to make their dreams a reality.

Persistent people *have a relentless desire to achieve their goals*. You have probably met people that have a list of things they want to accomplish. There are also people who not only want to achieve their goals, but fervently do so. They can do anything and go to any lengths to achieve their goals.

Persistent people *are confident about what they want from life*. They came to this realization at a young age it became entrenched in their personality. As mentioned earlier, persistent people go after their goals hungrily. They know what they want and do not change their views for anything or anyone.

Persistent people *develop their habits at an early age*. In all honesty, they are not like ordinary people. They recognize the value of persistence and self-discipline while striving to maintain it throughout their lives. They believe the results of their outcome will be apparent in the long run.

Persistent people *do not waste their time with plans and activities that do not push them closer to their goals*. They are quick to adapt, adjust, and make required changes in their plans and strategies. They are not afraid of change and continue adjusting throughout their journey to success.

Meeting Management Skills

Want to know what it takes to have successful and productive meetings?

Meeting management skills have never been in as high demand as they are now. This can be attributed to people becoming more interactive. Unfortunately, this interaction can be dangerous if not directed towards useful means. As a result, meetings are an essential part of a company.

Managers hold meetings with their teammates to discuss new initiatives, plans, procedures and goals that need to be achieved. Project managers arrange meetings with other managers to discuss the strategy and risk factors associated with every desired outcome.

Why Is It So Important To Develop Meeting Management Skills?

If you do not know how to manage a team, you cannot reap the benefits of scaling your business. Often in many work environments, people are unable to work to their full potential because they are not given proper training and/or complete guidance by their supervisors and managers. Meetings serve the core purpose of communicating these responsibilities and expectations. As such, they need to be managed properly.

What Are The Key Factors Of Effective Meeting Management?

Before going to a meeting or arranging one, it is important that you have a documented form of all discussion topics. You might think that you will remember all the important points to be discussed. However, once the meeting starts and everyone begins talking you will likely forget your points. To be on the safe side and reap all the benefits, have an outline of your main topics and issues.

Be prepared to open your meeting with the areas that are functioning properly. Give any good news first, acknowledge team members that have excelled, share stats that have grown, etc. Then follow up with the areas that need improving and open it up for discussion. Allow for solutions to come from the team even if you may have a strategy in mind. Look for ways to incorporate some of the suggestions that were made and be prepared to close the meeting on a positive note.

Provide equal opportunities for each attendee to express himself or herself. There may be some people who are more eager to contribute because they have a lot to say, while others may be a little more reserved. People who are shy, especially women, often do not get an equal opportunity to speak. As a leader, it will be your responsibility to allocate the time fairly to all attendees and listen carefully to what they have to say.

Having a documented meeting agenda will also help press for closure and avoid any possible confusion or conflicts. Take each agenda one by one and before moving to the next point, make sure that you have clarified what will be done and who will be doing it.

It is also important to protect the less assertive people from more dominant employees who may attempt to take more time to share. This is important because the time should be spent on ensuring everyone knows their responsibilities and duties.

Summarizing the discussed points and the entire meeting is as important as writing a conclusion to an essay or article. Do you know what will happen if you keep moving from point to point without a strong summary? It will not be effective, which means your time will be wasted. Summarize the points, things that need to be done, people responsible for them, and actions plans.

Keeping record of each meeting is important and will act as a guide for you and team members. The best way to keep a record and ensure that everyone is clear about their role and duties is by distributing the meeting minutes within 24 hours. Ask them to review the minutes from the meeting and get back to you if they need to clarify anything. This way the outcomes of the meeting will be effective.

Personal And Professional Development

You should never stop adding to your personal and professional development skills. The best way to do your job is by learning new things. Did you know that every successful person has one habit in common?

That habit is, you guessed it, reading books. You might think that reading a book in a digital world is antiquated. Contrary to popular opinion, it keeps your mind in perfect condition and helps you learn new skills that you can apply in your business and personal life.

Let's take a B2B BREAK right here.

What are the key factors of personal and professional development skills?

_____
_____
_____
_____
_____

Make a separate list of your professional and personal development goals.

_____
_____
_____
_____
_____
_____
_____
_____

Now list at least 3 long term goals and break them into smaller goals.

_____
_____
_____
_____
_____

Make a separate plan for each small goal, the time span, and the method to achieve it.

_____
_____
_____
_____
_____
_____
_____
_____
_____
_____
_____
_____
_____
_____
_____
_____
_____
_____
_____
_____
_____
_____
_____
_____
_____

Look for transferrable skills that can be used in both personal and professional growth.

_____
_____
_____
_____

If you do not achieve your goals in a set time, determine where you went wrong, make changes, and start all over again.

Developing an appropriate skill set for your personal and professional life is a must, especially if you want to be successful in both spheres. Many people make their lists but fail to adhere to them. They procrastinate and wait to start the process once they have enough time and resources.

The best time to start anything is NOW, and you need to start today to have an impactful tomorrow.

Write a list of your skill set for your own personal and professional life.

_____
_____
_____
_____
_____
_____
_____
_____
_____
_____
_____

Brand To Bucks

Your Stuff

Every business needs the proper set of items that keep it running smoothly. This is crucial for the success of every organization. View your business as a big machine. What does a machine require to stay functional?

First, the right kind of parts. Second, the parts should be in working condition and then placed in a system.

I remember being on a business webinar years ago and the guest speaker, Dee Marshall of the Girlfriends Pray movement, shared her big breakthrough story. She told us she got a call to speak at a major national conference and just before hanging up the phone the Coordinator said, "Hey, wait a minute! I have one more question. Do you happen to know of any other speakers?"

Dee went on to share with us that she had one of her girlfriends in mind for the job! All her friend had to do was email her headshot, a short biography and website to the Network Coordinator and she was IN!

To her surprise, when she called her girlfriend with the good news, her excitement was met with great disbelief. This friend had not one of the items needed to present to the coordinator. Dee was so upset. Then she said these words to us, "my friend missed this huge opportunity because she didn't have her STUFF together!"

How many people do you know that are "doing business" and have nothing to show for it? No proof that they are building a brand. Sometimes it is the small things that we fail to do in the beginning that can ruin us in the end.

To assure your brand success, first determine what kind of business materials you require and how to keep them in perfect condition. The process requires research, planning, and the right strategies to accomplish the task. As each of the machine's parts require proper oiling, each of the business materials require proper updating to stay fresh and relevant.

What Does Your Business Require?

Depending on the nature of your business, you may require a variety of items to consistently offer value and good service to your customers.

We will discuss some of the core business solutions necessary for every corporate entity. You will also learn some of the most effective ways to make your material even more engaging for your clients and customers.

Media

What exactly does your business require to function and run effectively?

- Business Emails
- Videos
- Ads, Social Media Campaigns
- Business Cards, Banners, Post Cards

Your website is the very first place where customers land and therefore, it serves as the face of your business. When you, or an outside source, design your website, you must incorporate and verify some key features.

- Proper graphics and formatting
- Content in line with your services and products
- Color scheme that complements the logo and the overall look of the website
- Optimized for search engines and customers

Once your website is created keep it fresh and updated. This will ensure high search engine rankings and encourage customers to visit your website frequently.

How do you keep your website fresh and updated for your business?

There is no universal method to accomplish this task, but there are some simple ways to periodically add content to your website and maintain a fresh look.

Have A Blog

Blogging is great for businesses and keeping your website updated with fresh content. Now this does not mean you have to blog daily. One or two posts per week will suffice.

Search engines give better rankings to sites that regularly add and update content because they receive new content while indexing. In addition, consistent blogging will solidify your reputation and demonstrate that you care about customers and clients.

Audit Your Website As A Visitor

Since you are a business owner, you may not understand how your website resonates with visitors. Try putting yourself in the shoes of your website's visitors.

Thoroughly review every aspect of your site. Review its content, color scheme, layout, user experience, etc. Then ask yourself these questions: Is it easy to navigate? Was the information easily accessible and displayed clearly?

If not, work on those areas. You can also browse other business sites for a point of reference. Learn how to improve your own site and incorporate new elements.

Incorporate A News Section

People want to know about you and your company's current events because they want to stay connected and informed. Incorporate a news section into your website to increase the number of pages and relay the most relevant, updated information.

Include topics such as charity events, partnerships with other companies, team meetings, company functions, upcoming products and services, etc.

Share a wealth of information with your customers because the more you share, the more they will feel connected to you and your website. Your website will also stay fresh and updated in the process.

Add Images And Videos

Visual content is great for generating traffic, marketing your business, and keeping your website professional and up to date for new visitors.

Add images of recently completed projects, new store arrivals, and upload videos that demonstrate how to use your products. You can also add tutorials to your site.

By regularly updating your site with new information, you will increase traffic and gain new customers.

Add Testimonials

Client testimonials are great for displaying successful projects and skills that you have used to help your clients. Testimonials show new visitors that you are reliable and capable of addressing their needs.

In addition to testimonials, you can add more menu pages to your website. More pages mean more content and more content means that you will have better search engine rankings. If your business is more interactive with customers, consider adding a section with staff profiles.

Business Email

Business email, or email marketing, is a great way to stay in touch with customers and keep track of their requirements.

Carefully planned, crafted, and implemented email marketing strategies will keep you ahead of the competition and ensure that your customers remember you. Once you have created a list of clients and customers, you should focus on ways to regularly stay in touch. Email marketing is a perfect way to stay connected with clients and customers.

What Types Of Emails Should Be Used In Your Email Marketing Campaign?

No matter what industry you work in, you should send these five types of emails to stay in touch with your customers and establish an effective relationship:

Promotional Emails

Promotional emails are used to promote different products and services. These emails should not be lengthy; they're normally short and engaging. You can also be creative with these emails by adding graphics to make them more visually pleasing.

New Arrivals Emails

These emails are useful for informing customers about new products and services you have added to your store or business. It is a two-fold process; you are promoting these products while guiding customers to purchase them.

To make the process more appealing, include pictures of newly added products along with catchy product descriptions showing its features and benefits.

Email Newsletter

This is one of the most important features of your content marketing campaign. Newsletters are used to inform customers about your company's current events and provide them with useful information related to your business.

A company newsletter will help you establish a strong relationship with your customers by delivering value and fostering trust.

Product Advice Emails

These emails are used to educate customers about using your products. The best way to consistently use these emails is by making a series of emails and sending them on a weekly or bi-weekly basis.

Survey Emails

You cannot serve without knowing your aim and what is expected of you. You should know if you are performing well.

Get feedback from your customers by sending survey emails and encouraging them to participate. Use the collected data to improve your services and repeat the process after a few months.

Types Of Videos You Should Add To Your Business

Business Videos

People love visual content because it is an easy way to understand and digest information. It is a powerful marketing tactic that engages the audience and increases traffic.

Videos are well-regarded because they are lively and offer a more personal experience not possible with written content.

In addition, videos have become increasingly influential in generating sales. More and more customers rely on videos to make important purchase decisions.

The following are the top three types of videos every business should have:

Explainer Videos

Every business should have an explainer video on their website. An explainer video tells visitors about the unique qualities and operations of your business. People want information immediately and an explainer video will quickly inform visitors about your business.

Product Demonstration Videos

How will visitors know how to use your products, or you are giving them premium, quality services? Simple; your product demonstration videos. Every time you upload a new product, upload a 'How-to' video alongside it. Videos are great for increasing website traffic.

Client Testimonial Videos

Testimonial videos let visitors know your business is trustworthy. If your clients and customers are also featured in the videos, the visitors will have an even greater interest in your business.

To make these videos, you will first need the permission of your clients and customers. Arrange the video recording sessions by having a professional resource available.

Media

Social media campaigns are some of your most useful business tools. You have probably heard this expression repeatedly, "if you are not online, you don't exist."

While the digital world has made it easier to reach and connect with people worldwide, it has made the promotional process much more difficult.

In previous years, when the internet was new, businesses could easily gain prominence. Now that the culture has increased to tremendous levels, everyone is online.

Businesses literally fight and compete with other businesses to build a reputation and gain more followers.

People have numerous choices. To ensure you are their choice, you must implement a carefully drafted social media campaign.

Essentials Of A Successful Social Media Campaign

To make a successful and productive social media campaign, you must first take the time ask yourself the following question.

What Do You Want To Achieve? Simply saying you want a huge following is way too vague. Shrewd businesses know their social media campaigns are as important as any other system or process. How will their audience learn about them if they are unaware they exist?

Let's take a B2B BREAK right here.

Ok you may be thinking I can barely keep up with one social media platform! Listen I feel your pain! Take a deep breath! You do not have to implement all this information right away, but I want you to think about what you can do TODAY.

What can you commit to doing to serve your customers? Here is a list of the goals I generally want to achieve with my social media campaigns. Pick at least 3.

- Gain new visitors to my site
- Gain new customers
- Increase your brand awareness
- Reinforce your business story
- Improve consumer communication and interaction

Before we move forward, list 3 goals you would like to accomplish:

_____
_____
_____
_____
_____
_____
_____

_____
_____
_____
_____
_____

Now list the tasks required to accomplish those goals:

_____
_____
_____
_____
_____
_____
_____
_____
_____
_____

Set a timeline of when you would like to see these goals accomplished:

_____
_____
_____
_____

Who Are You Serving?

In simple terms, who are the customers and potential customers you want to attract and obtain? Without a clear picture of the kind of people you want to associate with, you will be lost amongst the crowd. If you want to serve better, know them better.

Before making an offer, generate a list of potential customers' characteristics and research them. Determine their likes, dislikes, and the content and products that interest them.

Having all the information about your potential/ideal customers will allow you to design an appropriate strategy for your business.

What Are Your Competitors Doing?

Researching your ideal competitors is important. Let me say for the record, this is not an area where you need to devote a lot of time.

Serving your customers should always be your focus. You must know their needs and their pain points. Solving their problems should always be your number one goal.

I personally do not believe you should simply duplicate what your competition does without an understanding of "why" they do what they do. Knowing the "why" may position you to be able to come up with a more suitable and beneficial service and/or product than your competitors currently offer.

Keeping an eye on your competitors is important because you all are working in the same business sphere. You need to know their potential next steps. One of the best ways to stay ahead of your competitors is to stay abreast of the latest technologies, trends, and the market gap. When you know all of this, you will have an edge over your competitors.

Specifically, you will know where your customers are headed, how their habits and preferences are changing, and what you offer that your competitors lack.

Be careful not to get too consumed with those you are in competition with and miss out on listening to the needs of your customers.

Another advantage of having your eyes open and knowing your competitors is that you will learn from their mistakes and successes. You can use this acquired knowledge to formulate your content and marketing strategies.

Your Content Calendar

Want to drive more traffic and sales? Content is a must for every business. Not just any type of content, we are talking about quality content that offers and dispenses value to readers.

If you think that social media strategies should not be included in your work schedule, then you should rethink your position.

What will you share with your followers, fans, and other business connections if you lack proper content? Strong content allows your potential customer the data needed to form an opinion about your brand.

Every engagement, every impression can shorten the sales funnel process, gradually turning a NO in to a resounding YES! There are endless types of content you can choose from, here are a few:

- Blogs – Written content
- Vlogs – Video content
- Infographics – Imagery w. minimal text
- Unboxing Videos – Influencers unboxing products for their followers
- Podcasts – Audio content
- eBooks – Written content

- Lists – List of tips, tricks, what to do, what to avoid, etc...
- Surveys – Statistics and studies
- Emails – Electronic correspondence containing updates, coupons, videos, etc…

Make a list of the mediums you will add to your strategy, and plan what will be posted every week. Your content should tell a story. The best brands do just that!

Think of your brand as a large book, what is the overall moral of your story? Who are the main characters? Where does the story take place? What is the problem and the solution? Tell your story, develop content that shares the pages out of your brand's book.

What's The Budget?

How Many Promotional Mediums Come In Your Budget?

While writing articles, posting them on your blog and sharing them across your social media platforms is relatively inexpensive. There are several promotional methods that require some reasonable financial investment on your part. Some mediums include:

- Pay Per Click (PPC) Campaigns
- Email Marketing Campaigns
- Affiliates Campaigns
- Radio, television, and print advertisements

If you want to incorporate any or all the aforementioned modes of advertising, then have a reasonable budget allocated for it. It is not necessary to use multiple modes; you can also choose a specific one based on your business' needs and budget.

What Kind Of Business Cards Will Make Them Call You?

Your business cards are essential for engaging with other businesses and helping them get in touch with you. Companies spend thousands of dollars on marketing, promotion, and making useful connections with the help of various channels.

However, only a few of them identify the power of good and influential business cards.

How many times have you received a business card and disposed of it right away?

Many times, probably. There are many reasons why people, including yourself, might toss a business card straight into the trash bin. Your best bet to avoid this situation is by learning from others' mistakes.

To be great, you should read about great people. Hence, if you want to avoid mistakes, you should learn from others and their mistakes. So, what kinds of business cards have the potential to make your potential clients call you?

Cards With Good Size

Size is an important aspect of a business design and serves as a key element to help you make a lasting impression on the card recipients. The usual size for a business card is 3.5 x 2 but why not supersize it?

Unconventional things stand out because they grab your attention. Larger cards will showcase the design of your card and make your contact details more visually appealing. It will compel a second look from your potential clients, which increases the chances for contact.

Cards With Unusual Shapes

Now we all know that a business card has a rectangular or square shape, so how about playing around with it? Much like size, you can break away from the usual shapes of a business card. Look around and see what you can use for inspiration that will also reflect your business.

Some Examples Include
- Key shaped design for your real estate business card
- Desserts design for your creamery or desserts business
- Shape of a blush box for your cosmetic industry

There are many more examples to choose from. Just see what fits your business brand and transform it into your next business card design.

Cards With Minimal Design And Colors

Vibrant colors and amalgam graphics are flashy but lack substance. A card with these designs may be successful in grabbing attention but not in a positive way. Potential clients and customers will see it, give it a second look, and then toss it into the bin.

Basically, it is game over. If you want to stay professional, adhere to the 'less is more' notion and keep colors and designs minimal.

Cards With Complete Details

How will your clients contact you if you have not mentioned complete and appropriate information on your business cards? A good business card, with all your creativity ingrained, will have:

- Your complete name
- Your business' complete name
- Your professional email addresses
- Your office/work phone number
- Website Address
- Social Media Handles

All your amazing designs and creative work will be in vain if your card does not have the complete contact details.

Products And Services

How Can You Determine The Products And Services To Sell?

Coming up with the right product can be as difficult as designing it. The wrong product can ruin your reputation and business, while the right product can potentially bring loads of benefits.

You are mistaken if you believe you can come up with any product and make it a success. It does not work like that. Many businesses make the mistake of not doing their homework before launching a product and face the consequences afterwards.

To make your products and services a success with customers, you should consider the following three things:

The Need

Products that are like existing ones do not have the same effect as ones that are different, act differently, and offer benefits to the customers.

While choosing a product, do a market research and see whether your product is in demand. Research your ideal customers and see what they require. Ponder over their buying habits and if your product passes the test, it is good to go.

Knowing Your Competition

People gravitate to products that have high competition because they are easy to develop, launch, and market. They simply ride the wave of what is trending. There are great products that require more effort to get off the ground, but they yield longer lasting results.

This is because they have less competition, which means you must lay a stronger foundation and take the time to educate your audience on the product or service you offer. There will be minimal to no businesses focusing on it and this will give you leverage over them.

The Unique Selling Point

Now comes the most important question: Why should I listen to you and buy from you? If your product is already unique, then the answer will be simple; describe the features and benefits.

On the other hand, if you have competition then you will need to elaborate on the ways your product will benefit your customers and why it is better than existing ones.

Let's take a B2B BREAK right here.

Do You Know Your Competition?

How much competition is out there for your product or service? List them.

_____
_____
_____
_____
_____

Which of those listed above do you have to directly compete with to gain prominence? (Ex: Similar brands in close proximity, strongest on-line presence, etc.)

_____
_____
_____
_____
_____

What makes you different? Make a list of unique features and benefits that your products offer.

_____
_____
_____
_____
_____
_____
_____

Based on the list above design a content campaign around them.

_____
_____
_____
_____
_____
_____
_____
_____
_____

What media platforms would you use to share the campaign listed above?

_____
_____
_____
_____

Well-maintained and updated business "stuff" will successfully sustain you for years. Having an updated website and other business materials will show your company is diligent, consistent, and concerned with keeping everything in working condition. So, get your stuff together!

Your System

Now that you have an idea of the "stuff" you need, there must be a system in place for each area. Think about it, our world is made up of systems. Your body runs systematically, our cars run systematically, our electricity runs systematically, our entire universe operates on a system!

Trust me, you cannot run your business without a system in place. So, for all my 'fly by the seat of my pants' entrepreneurs this chapter may give you a bit of a headache.

Every successful business is made up of several operational systems that keep it running smoothly and in perfect condition. As stated earlier, your business is no less than a machine and requires each of its parts to work in a perfect condition for proper functioning.

Like everything else, different businesses can have different operations and systems based on their requirements and needs. However, there are some systems that are universal. The following systems are essential for every business as most cannot survive without them.

Many of you may not be aware that your business' backend is the place that brings in most of the big sales. The marketing and sales system are made up of two parts: the frontend and the backend.

The frontend marketing is the hub of most activities such as searching for new customers and clients, explaining the features and benefits of your services and products, making them believe your offer is the perfect solution to their needs and finally, taking them to the point of making the sale. It includes all the promotional activities like banners, brochures, and other marketing actions.

The backend is the foundational part of a business and comprises a large portion of your operating system. The backend contains all the company's technologies, content management system, and ERP (Enterprise Resource Planning) to keep customer information safe and secure. The backend also consists of your loyal customers data which makes up most of your major repeat sales and keeps your business running smoothly.

Key Operational Systems

What Are The Key Operational Systems Of Your Business?

To have a strong frontend business, you should build a strong and concrete backend system. People do not come across the backend section of your business, but they can easily judge and identify its condition from their viewpoint and experience.

At the beginning of every new year I pull my team together to teach a course called *90 Days to Dominate*. We dive into key areas that can make or break entrepreneurs from Finances and Team Building to Emotional Intelligence.

I am hell bent on making certain all the students walk away with something that can increase their bottom line once applied to their business practices.

In our 2018 class I discussed the importance of putting systems in place, it was overwhelming for some because many have a skeleton crew doing all the work.

They are the CEO, the CFO and the COO all in one! I dived into the C-Suite roles and discussed the importance of finding key persons that oversee different areas of your business. *You cannot do it all.*

An efficient and effective operational system prevents poor brand performance. Therefore, planning and keeping it updated and functional is essential. Here are a *few* key operational systems:

- Marketing System
- Sales System
- Payment System
- Customer Relationship Management (CRM) System
- Human Resource System
- Customer Support System
- Hiring &Training System
- Social Media System

Your Marketing System

Every business should have a perfectly tailored marketing system to function properly. It is essential you have a plan designed and implemented at the earliest stage of business. Marketing can be tiresome and time consuming; you must find new customers, make use of various social media channels, and drive traffic using several marketing strategies.

Once a business starts, every businessperson is sure about what he or she wants from it, their motivations, and their reasons for operating the business in a field. This sounds good, but this is not enough.

Do you know that many businesses fail due to the lack of a clearly defined promotional plan? You need to market your business appropriately if you want more traffic and customers for your site.

How Can You Have An Effective Marketing Plan?

An effective marketing plan is one designed around a business' needs and requirements. A good marketing and promotional plan will have the following things:

Clearly Defined Goals List:
- Strengths, Weakness, Opportunities, and Threats (SWOT) and Political, Economic, Social, & Technological (PEST) analysis of the business to identify the opportunities and risks of the business in all possible ways
- Mediums through which products and services will be marketed
- Modes and methods for how goals will be attained in a specific time frame
- A mix of the 4 P's of marketing (Product, Price, Place, & Promotion) to segment and sell the products and services to different social sectors
- Evaluation, changes, and repetition.

Remember if it cannot be measured it cannot be managed. The only way to know a system is working is to check the data, the numbers. Every marketing plan should increase the opportunity for sales to be considered successful.

Your Sales System

The sales process can be both confusing and complex for many businesses. A common misconception is that the sales process does not require any planning and runs all on its own. It is nothing like this. To have complete control over the system and keep it in running condition, you must have a properly defined and planned sales process.

Do You Have An Effective Sales Process?

Sales is the cash flow generating portion of any business transaction. You need to use wisdom while strategizing your sales process because a single wrong step can ruin the entire process. Here are seven steps you want to incorporate into your sales strategy:

Clearly Defining The Benefits

You should know about your products, its features, and how it benefits your potential customers. Talking about the features is not enough. Tell them specifically how you can add value to their life with your products and/or services.

Find Your Customers

If you think everyone is your client, then no one is your client! Identify who is a match for your type of business. Look for your potential customers through different modes with social media at the top of the list. Make your social profiles and connect with people that can be your ideal customers. Start the relationship with casual conversation and please refrain from making an offer right away.

Build Trust

Identify the requirements of your customers. They should be the focus of your business and to cater to them, you should know about their wants, needs and problems.

Ask carefully crafted questions to know about their preferences and requirements and make the offer accordingly. Questions that yield a "YES" as an answer, and require minimal explanation are ideal. Exercise patience, a positive tone, a confident and professional disposition.

Presentation Matters

Present your products and/or services in a way that is appealing to the customer. Remember this is all about experience. Any wrong step can delay closing a sale. Show them how well it suits their needs along with the benefits. As stated before, talking about features is not enough. Talk about the benefits your customers can expect.

Call To Action

Once you have sufficiently built a comfortable relationship with them, it is time to make the offer. Gather all the information about your products and/or services and converse with your ideal customers. You can also cold call them to let them know about your offer.

Close

After you have made your offer and the client has agreed to it, you need to make a winning close. Otherwise, your client will hang in the air thinking about the next step. Guide them and ask when you can deliver the product to their office or company.

Follow Up

A great follow up is essential for great long-lasting customer relationship. This is also essential if you want to build your sales funnel for repeat business.

Your Payment System

There are many opportunities during your brand experience to leave a positive, lasting impression on your customer. Your payment system is another area which can accomplish this.

First and foremost, you want to make the process as simple as possible. No one wants to go through a time-consuming process of filling out long and detailed forms when purchasing an item.

If you want to have more traffic, customers, and sales, make the very last process of your system simple and easy for your customers to use and checkout.

How To Have An Effective Payment And Checkout System

Follow the steps below to integrate an effective and easy payment process into your website:

Multiple Payment Modes

Instead of sticking to a single mode of payment, it is better to offer multiple modes of payment so that the customer can choose the one that is suitable for them. However, you can have a single mode. Still, people like it when they are given freedom to decide.

Quick And Convenient

Do not ask for too much information. Stick to the basics and say that you need to process the payment.

Do not ask them to sign up to make the payment. People already have a number website id and the thought of requiring another one for checkout will dissuade them.

Safe And Secure

Guarantee that their credit details and other personal details will be kept safe and you take privacy matters seriously.

Whenever there is an error, a wrong postal code or phone number, do not place the pop-up all the way up on the form. Make it appear on the field that requires correction.

Popular Payment Systems

Some Payment Systems you can check out are PayPal, Etsy, Square, Stripe, Moon Clerk, etc... You can also research Credit Card Processing Companies and see if their software is a fit for your websites shopping cart.

Your CRM System

Customer Relationship Management (CRM) is an approach to managing a company's interaction with current and future customers. It often involves using technology to organize, automate, and synchronize sales, marketing, customer service, and technical support.

Businesses spend thousands of dollars to have effective CRM software for their businesses and companies. In order to make the investment work, however, it requires time and effort. Many businesses, even after spending their hard-earned cash on CRM software, are unable to get the desired results from their system. This is because they believe this step is finished and does not require additional work.

Have An Effective CRM System

The following are some ways to make your CRM system productive:

Make it easy for your employees to use. After all, they will be the ones using it and if it is too hard for them, how will they use it effectively?

Train all your employees to use the installed CRM. Conduct once a week training to make sure that all your employees know how to use and handle the system.

Do not treat it as a standalone sales automation system. Be sure to integrate all your company's departmental systems into it. Use it to track your customers' behavior throughout the entire sales process. From the beginning to the end, keep track of where they are going, which phone they are using, what kind of content they share, and the social platforms they use to gather useful customer information.

Integrate it with your social media platforms and profiles. It is a great way to keep track of where your potential customers are going and posting. You generally receive social profiles associated with the email address entered by the visitor.

Keep all the information entered and saved in the CRM in a proper and up-to-date manner. Your system will be of no benefit if it has outdated information. Current customer data prevents your sales representatives from having to re-enter the information again.

Some of the most popular CRM Systems are Hub Spot, Zoho, Sales Force, Infusion Soft, etc. Research and see what system is best for your company.

Your Human Resource Management System

If you want to have a successful and functioning business, then having a quality human resource management (HRM) system should be your primary goal. While there is no shortage of talented and quality people that can work within your corporate culture, there can be a lack of ability to identify these people.

The common belief is that good employees are rather difficult to find, and it takes more than just a good comp package to retain them.

You must understand that talented, experienced employees are never lacking opportunities, even when there is a job shortage. HRM is one of the building blocks that strengthens a company by helping recruit and retain the best talent.

I first stepped out into entrepreneurship as a hair stylist at the age of 19. I paid a monthly booth rent at a salon, which meant I was responsible for building my clientele.

I had no idea it would be as difficult as it was to build my business. It was not until my friend from Beauty School, Melissa Scott, called me to see how I was doing and told me she was working at a salon chain.

She went on to tell me about the training classes they offered and their salary with health benefits. I did not make the move right away but after relocating to several salons paying booth rent without success, I decided to go for it.

I walked into their downtown Orlando location and interviewed with their manager, named Laura. I was so nervous, I did not have experience cutting men's hair, which was a majority of their clientele.

But when she heard about my journey in this business thus far and my age she was impressed. She saw something in me I was not privy to. It was a few years later, after having my first son, that I sat in Laura's office again and she talked to me about training for management.

That was one of the single monumental events that led me to managing a salon, on to becoming the youngest District Manager overseeing 6 locations, 6 managers and 70+ employees. I was a good hire for Laura! Your ability to hire, research, and ask the right questions can make or break your organization.

How To Effectively Manage Your HR System

Listed below are some of the most effective ways of managing your HRM:

Team Training

Train your HRM team to deal with employees in an effective manner. One of the mistakes most businesses make is to see training unnecessary for experienced staff.

It is taught not caught! Your company's culture, systems, core beliefs will not rub off vicariously! Even newly hired, talented, experienced staff members need to know the details about your company's vision and core beliefs.

Training will help them understand their roles and responsibilities within the company. In my own experience, if Laura only looked at my skill sets to determine if I was a candidate for the job, I would not have been hired. Her confidence was in the training courses that would follow to get my skill sets to where they needed to be. Give your team the tools to win!

Be Fair

Provide equal opportunities to everyone. People are smart and if they sense that you are showing favoritism to certain employees, they will start looking for other job opportunities. Trust me, it will not take them long to find another job. Equality is a must if you want to have the best people on your team.

Offer Incentives

Keeping employees motivated and their productivity on high gear can be a daunting task and must be addressed at the very first sign of low performance.

Keep them motivated by providing better and satisfying packages, activities that help them destress, and training that helps them develop new skills. Reward and recognize them for a job well done.

Open Communication

Communication is the key to better and long-lasting relationship. Without knowing what is bothering your employees and hindering their progress, you will not be able to come up with effective solutions. As a result, your employees may start resenting you.

Provide A Safe Workplace

Having a strong anti-harassment policy is important for your business and your employee's safety and peace of mind. Do you think they will be able to fully focus on their work if they feel unsafe? Having some flexibility is good but not in the case of your company's harassment policies.

Depending on the size of your company you may be wearing the hat of HR. This role can be outsourced, do not be afraid to seek out professional help in this or any area.

Let's take a B2B BREAK right here.

Take a deep breath.

This section, for a lot of new entrepreneurs, can be hard to take in. You will hear me say often, just because you know how to make the cake does not mean you can run the bakery.

You may not be in the hiring phase of your business or looking for a CRM, but it is a goal you should set as you expand.

What system(s) do you want to work on next in your business?

_____

_____

_____

_____

How can you improve your hiring process?

_____
_____
_____
_____

What are some ways you can improve employee relations?

_____
_____
_____
_____

Does each employee know how to operate your current system, if not where is training needed?

_____
_____
_____
_____

Effective Backend Management System

There are several ways to help you improve your backend system. Adding the following components will increase its efficacy:

Train your salesperson to interact with customers patiently and effectively. There may come times when your customers act impatiently. Train your staff to handle such situations. They should also guide them in the purchasing process and tell them about other products.

Make a content strategy to keep the backend customers in the loop. Since they will buy from you more readily than from a new person, make sure you send them an email to earn a quick profit.

Content strategy includes newsletters, auto responders, new product emails, and occasionally, some free gifts like eBooks or reports that are of value to them.

Make a list of the customers in your CRM that have moved to the back-funnel area of your business and design products exclusively for them. You can also mention it in the email and tell them how it can benefit them.

Ask for feedback from customers. Do not hesitate to call them, email them, or ask them during the purchase process about their experience. This will ensure they recommend you to others. Collect the data and use it to improve your services and products further.

If you want to move your frontend customers to the back-funnel sales and retain the backend customers, then make it a point to answer their questions and queries as quickly as possible. They will come to you if they have any issues with your products or services and expect you to help them. They will remember and trust you if you give them what they need.

Strongly integrated systems make strong business; it strengthens the business and keeps it in working condition. While there will be times when you will forget about maintenance, a good and strong system requires proper care to function flawlessly.

Schedule the time for maintenance, check for corks or system errors, look for areas where automation can be implemented. The goal is to have a system that helps you serve your customers and employees; it makes for a happy work environment.

Customer Service

Customers are the lifeline of any business. Good customer service is a necessity if you want your business to outshine your competitors. Having remarkable customer service is necessary regardless of the size of the organization.

Large organizations have big budgets that allow them to have a fully specialized customer care staff small businesses lack. Mom and Pop businesses can get overlooked unless they have something more to offer than those huge brands. A small business has something big businesses rarely offer better and interactive customer service.

Your Customer Support System

Customers are essential for a business. Cash is also essential for a business and customers are the source of that cash. A good customer support system (CRM) is an integral part of every company.

If you want to have repeat customers, repeat sales, loyal customers, and a good market reputation, then invest in your customer support.

No matter what business you are in, if you want to stay successful, make your customer support operations better. Like larger companies you want to be prepared to provide online reviews, surveys, and quicker response times on emails.

Be certain to have your team equipped to handle complaints. The ability to effectively solve your customers dissatisfaction can turn them into a loyal, lifetime customer.

How To Have An Effective Customer Support System

While planning your CRM, consider the following points to increase its effectiveness:

Hire the right kind of people for the job. Your human resource team may receive tons of applications for the job, but they need to select only the best and the most appropriate ones. If you are unsure of who can be a good addition to your customer support team, call them for an interview and give them a practical test.

Train your customer support team to keep the system running smoothly. Define their job responsibilities and duties during the training session. Assess their performance on a regular basis and in case of any deficiencies, arrange for sessions that will help them overcome shortcomings.

Provide them with a peaceful environment and perfect working equipment. You would not want to hear someone say they lost a client because there was an issue in the system, would you? Have all the systems checked regularly so any issues or technical problems will be encountered early on.

Train them to use your CRM system in a proper and effective manner so they will know how to keep record of all the clients without having to enter the same information again.

Answer their queries in a timely manner. Your employees are your internal customers and to keep them happy and satisfied, you should address their issues in a timely and satisfactory manner. You cannot interact with your customers by yourself, at least not all the time. Your customer support team is the face of your company, and they will keep your clients satisfied if they are happy themselves.

Your Hiring System

Where marketing enables you to design and implement useful promotional strategies for success, human resources keep your employees motivated and verify that customer support ensures your employees are happy and satisfied. Your hiring system makes sure that you have the best people for all these positions. Before starting your talent hunt, it is important to have well-defined hiring policies and job descriptions.

Clear job descriptions will help you and potential employees make the right decisions and avoid any future and possible conflicts. Since you will hire people for your company, you should inform them of policies, expectations and benefits. Spend a reasonable amount of time explaining and highlighting all this information.

How To Have An Effective Hiring System

Making your hiring plan can be complex and time-consuming. You may be tempted, to throw everything aside and make a hire. But it is best to take the time to ensure you are hiring the best person for the job. The following factors will help you devise a beneficial hiring policy:

Choose the board of interviewers carefully. Many people think that conducting an interview is easy, but this is a misconception.

During the interview, the people conducting it will be expected to assess the candidates on multiple levels. How will they accomplish this without any prior knowledge about the process? Train your interviewers beforehand. Make sure the people on the hiring board are qualified and know about the process thoroughly. You may want to add anyone or everyone from the management team, that have the right skills for the job and can ask the right questions.

A compensation plan is an integral part of a hiring policy and you may be tempted to add many things to it to hire good talent. Before making any additions, make sure they are fiscally responsible and in budget.

Make it a point that all the candidates will be told about the status of their interview within a week or ten days. Many companies keep the candidates waiting until they are no longer interested in joining them at all.

Train your HR department to make effective and clear job descriptions. Standard Operating Procedures (SOP's) are required.

Clarity of roles make it easier for your employees to perform the tasks required. A good job description has all the necessary information that attracts a potential employee. Make sure everything is stated in a clear way, especially if you want to hook the right candidates. I will add leaving room for creativity is crucial to a thriving and productive environment. Set your non-negotiables and allow for freedom in your organization's framework.

Be prepared to provide new hires with non-competes and non-disclosure forms. When hiring, you want to protect your company's trade secrets and systems. These documents let your employees and subcontractors know you mean business.

Let's take a B2B BREAK right here.

Write down some of the best components of your own management system(s).

_____
_____
_____

Write down some of the components of your own management system(s) that need improvement.

_____
_____
_____

Write a list of some of the systems you would like to research.

_____
_____
_____

Based on your research which CRM looks like a fit for your business?

_____
_____
_____

Your Success

If you are anything like me, you glanced through this book and then went back to the beginning and took your time to implement as many elements you possibly could.

My husband and I have paid hundreds and sometimes thousands for coaching and courses that has taken us years to implement. This takes time. Building a successful business is not an overnight process.

It requires the right concept, the right timing, the right advertising, the right market, and the right team. Now you have your story selling down to a "T", you understand the importance of having both style and substance.

Your plans are in place for continued education. Mastering your skill set is always on your list of priorities. You have a system in place for the various areas of your business and you are ready to start bringing in the big bucks! But here are some sobering facts about small businesses that I think you should know.

According to the Small Business Administration (SBA), about two-thirds of businesses survive 2 years, half of all businesses will survive 5 years and one-third will survive 10.

The longer a company can stay in business the longer their survival rate. Most of the businesses that fail do so because of a lack of cash flow and planning.

Once I resigned, from the salon franchise I worked for, I took some time off to help my husband with his real estate business and to have our second child. We were also heavily involved in some philanthropic work. During this time house flipping had become popular.

We had several properties we were renting out, in hopes to sell but the housing market took a nosedive. We ended up with all these amazing properties and no cash flow. We did not plan for the market crash!

We did not have a safety net in place and long story short we had to foreclose on all our properties, close my husband's company and start from scratch.

We had everything in place, the team, the marketing, the great customer service, awesome homes, but not enough financial backing to carry us through the dry spell. One of my greatest verses in the bible calls money a defense! During those lean seasons I learned the importance of that statement!

Show Me The Money

As money is coming in and out of your business you can lose track of what is truly a profit and a loss. Therefore, it is important to have an appointed person to keep track of your expenses, your invoices, your books.

I meet way too many entrepreneurs that do not separate their personal and professional bank accounts, and it can all become one big blur. When the time comes to get a loan, they cannot provide the proper documentation to support their company's earnings. I always tell the ladies in my CEO Chick Network, **the top four professionals every entrepreneur needs:**

- ➢ Accountant/Bookkeeper
- ➢ Tax Preparer
- ➢ Attorney
- ➢ Financial Advisor

Data does not lie, bank accounts do not lie, the numbers do not lie! How you look on paper, MATTERS! Saving your money is very important, and building your credit is vital to being approved for business loans.

There are several factors considered to having a strong credit score, here is how it is broken up:
- ➢ 35% of your score is payment history, your ability to pay on time
- ➢ 30% of your score is credit utilization, this refers to the amount of credit available to you. For example, if you have a credit card limit of $100 you should not use more than $30
- ➢ 15% of your score is age of the credit history, how long have you been a borrower
- ➢ 10% of your score is new credit, recent credit cards or loans you have applied for
- ➢ 10% of your score is credit mix, such as utilities, phone bills, mortgages, medical, etc…

It is important to build up a savings for your business as well as your credit in case additional funding is needed.

Multiple Streams Of Income

No matter if you have a lucrative job or a great business, having an additional stream of income is always a good idea. Did you know that all successful people have secondary income sources to help support their main business?

They never rely on a single stream of income because they realize you can never be certain of anything. Your well-paying job or your perfectly run business can have multiple and potentially detrimental issues. A financial crisis is one of the most destructive concerns of a business.

Financial crisis is nothing new for businesses and many have faced it at some point in their journey. To keep your business up and running, you need capital and multiple sources to ensure that you are never short on finances.

Multiple sources of income also mean you will have a better financial status than many of your competitors. Many of them, more than likely, rely on a single business.

The money that comes from multiple sources can be used for various means. It would be wise to put the money in a savings account as well as an investment account.

Want to find a profitable income idea for your secondary income stream? It is not difficult to find ideas, but it is important that you choose wisely. For most you do not have to look far, there are ways to create various streams of income within your current business.

When I first launched CEO Chicks, we had one membership tier. As we grew and I became aware of the needs of my ideal customers and we added different levels. In the beginning we sold one style t-shirt, now we have various brand items for entrepreneurs to purchase. You can build on your products and services to increase your overall profit margins.

There are so many ways to produce other sources of income but again choose wisely because if you neglect this step, you will run the risk of wasting your time, effort and resources on something that is worthless.

Stay Consistent—Marketing And Content Schedule

After achieving a goal or reaching a satisfactory level, many businesses do not maintain what they worked so hard to create. This is disappointing because it can have dire consequences for your business and market reputation.

Stay consistent in driving your business forward. The goal is to always continue growing and earning. Break new records, go to new heights! The way to do this is by paying close attention to your marketing and content schedule. Marketing trends keep changing; things that are useful today may not be as effective tomorrow. Therefore, it is important to have all the updated and useful information.

The collected data will help you stay in line with your business' goals and incorporate the latest technologies into your strategies.

Disrupt The Market

What Should You Consider While Designing Your Marketing Plan?

A marketing plan is a crucial part of your business' foundation. It is important to ensure your business continues to function. When a business takes off on a successful path, it becomes easy to forget its purpose and the ideals behind its existence. A well-detailed marketing plan will be in line with your vision.

Moreover, a marketing plan will also help you gauge your progress and make the necessary changes to meet your goals. What are the essential factors of a detailed marketing plan?

Clearly defined goals. Why do you want to have a marketing plan and what do you want to achieve from it? Instead of making vague statements, it is better to specify your goals and establish a time frame to achieve them.

Conduct a detailed SWOT and PEST analysis of your businesses to identify the opportunities and possible bottlenecks that are likely to occur. The analysis will help you identify strengths, weaknesses, opportunities, and your business' scope in relation to cultural, economic, and social factors. SWOT = Strength, Weakness, Opportunities and Threats. PEST = Political, Economic, Socio-Cultural and Technological.

Research your audience and competitors thoroughly. See what motivates them and works best for them. The best way to do this is by following some of your competitors and seeing how they function. Make a map of your ideal customer and find ways to reach and connect with them.

After you have completed the research part, it is time to connect with them. But wait! Have you considered the mediums through which you will reach your audience? If yes, you can proceed. If not, then you have to stop and make a list of all the social mediums your ideal customers will utilize.

Lastly, plan and strategize your content accordingly. Content is the necessity of today's marketing and business world. The days when people used to survive without it are long gone. Integrate a blog into your website. Design a monthly editorial calendar and make sure it flows accordingly. It will help you improve your site's search engine rankings as well as establish a trustworthy reputation.

Memes

Memes are also very important for your marketing plan. The term, which was coined by Richard Dawkins in 1976, is essentially a "package of culture."

In terms of your business, memes can conveniently promote and package your business culture. Images with appropriate and attention-grabbing captions will ensure potential customers and clients will instantly recognize your business.

Since many memes have gone viral, this is an excellent way of growing the public's awareness of your business. Here are two examples of memes I have used for my own business:

Notice how the memes are clear, vibrant, and colorful? That's how your business memes should be. They need to stick in the minds of customers and show off your creativity. In turn, these customers will share your memes and they will potentially go viral. Make sure your captions stand out and that they convey whatever message you want customers to internalize.

Branding your memes will help to create a unique name and image for the product and/or service you provide. You want to engrain your business in the minds of customers through consistent and effective advertising campaigns.

Branding allows you to stand out from the competition while attracting and retaining loyal customers. Cultivating your brand through strong imagery will make potential and current customers immediately gravitate to your business.

There are many apps available for making memes. Canva, Spark Posts, Typorama, Word Swag are just a few. Give it a shot, be creative and have fun!

How To Make A Sale

Initially, I struggled in my business, but it was not until I developed my sales funnel I began to thrive. A sales funnel visually represents how a sale proceeds linearly from customer awareness to customer action.

Basically, a sales funnel demonstrates every sale starts with many potential customers and ends with a significantly smaller number of people who purchase your product and/or service.

Depending on the size and structure of your business, the sales funnel will vary. However, in general, sales funnels are divided into four sections:

- Awareness - people who are aware of a business
- Interest - people who have had contact with a business
- Desire - people who have repeated contact with a business
- Action - people who have made a purchase.

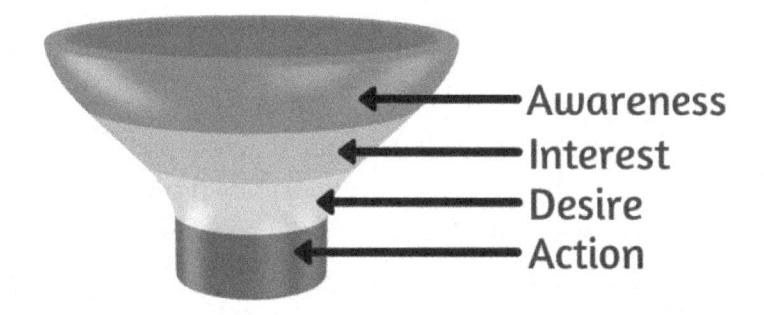

General Sales Funnel

- Awareness
- Interest
- Desire
- Action

28 Ways To Market Your Business:

There are several ways to market your business. While there are traditional methods, you may be doing now, I have listed some new and unconventional ways to promote your business.

1. Optimize your business website to get visibility in search engines
2. Create your Facebook page and group
3. Create other social media profiles to network with your clients
4. Use content marketing to build your tribe/following
5. Tell all the company people to join the social media pages
6. Have an exclusive LinkedIn profile
7. Encourage your audience to leave comments on your business profile
8. Put your business on Google Map
9. Be consistent with all the content across social platforms
10. Use Google+ to have a great business profile
11. Write fresh content and upload it on your website
12. Create a blog and post on it on a daily or weekly basis
13. Focus on visual content and strong imagery that defines your brand message
14. Make explainer/educational videos pertaining to your brand and post them on Vimeo, YouTube, Facebook, Instagram (short versions allowed @60seconds)
15. Invest in press releases for events
16. Promote your services by giving something of value for free (eBook, list of tips, etc…)
17. Use HubSpot to sell and promote your products
18. Write engaging classified ads and post them on various sites
19. Integrate a well-detailed and planned email marketing campaign in your business
20. Give free coupons as a gift to new customers

21. Make use of Google AdWords and other Pay Per Click (PPC) programs
22. Promote your business through eBay
23. Promote your business through Amazon and Flickr
24. Write an eBook about your business
25. Make a weekly or daily podcasting schedule for your business
26. Crowd funding is great; use it for your business promotion
27. Join various forums and interact with other people, especially bloggers
28. Guest blog for top sites

Let's take a B2B BREAK right here.

How much money can you start setting aside for your business savings?

_____
_____
_____
_____

What are some other products and services you can create to bring in additional streams of money?

_____
_____
_____
_____

Do you know your credit score? What is it? Create a plan to bring your debt down (google Dave Ramsey, Financial Peace)

_____
_____
_____
_____

What images would best describe your brand story?

_____
_____
_____
_____

What types of memes would you like to create to add to your content calendar? What would it say?

_____
_____
_____
_____

Develop Successful Habits For Life

Habits define you and help you define your life. All successful people work through their habits, building around their strengths and staffing their weaknesses. Many of these people believe success is all about earning and they share a single goal: to earn more.

This statement is true to some extent. After all we, all want to live comfortably, and this is no exception as an entrepreneur. However, did you know that they achieve their goals while staying consistent and presentable at the same time?

Many of them live long, happy and healthy lives in the process. They know that success not only requires hard work and dedication, but also requires a set of healthy and steady habits. They master those successful habits and stick to them until they become second nature

What are those habits that keep them going and set them apart from others? We have compiled a list of the top ten habits that are common in all successful CEOs. Learn and practice these habits to have a more fulfilling and successful life.

#1- They Exercise

Yes, we know that it sounds like old fashioned advice but come on! How do you think they manage to work for insanely long hours and still manage to show up polished and fresh?

It is because they have kept their most important tool in healthy condition: their body. Exercise is the very first habit that is practiced by many successful people, not just the famous CEOs. Look around and you will find similar people, who are leading successful lives, are strict about exercise.

Exercise keeps your body and mind in a healthy condition and allows it to endure severe conditions. Plus, you will live longer, which leads to more opportunities and achievements.

#2- They Eat Right

They are not the type of people who just grab anything when they are hungry. This habit goes hand in hand with the first one. Exercise alone can work wonders for your body and mind, but when paired with a proper diet, you are sure to function at your best consistently.

Instead of eating junk food, they prefer to replenish with fresh fruits and vegetables that prepare them for harder tasks. So, the next time you think about grabbing a piece of cake, remind yourself of your goals.

Having healthy eating habits does not mean they, or you, cannot have fun or eat out. You can still indulge, but it is important to strike a balance.

#3- They Plan Ahead

Another piece of advice and habit you must be familiar with is planning. Planning saves a lot of time and allows you to focus on the most important things first. Instead of starting your day slow, plan for what you will accomplish tomorrow so you can jump right into productivity.

Successful people have recognized the importance of planning early in their lives. Many of them even actually wrote down all their goals.

Think of it this way; everyone has goals in their lives, but some identify them earlier than others. Make sure to identify your goals immediately. Plan how you will achieve those goals and start your journey as soon as possible.

#4- They Meditate

People have a lot of thoughts, activities, and responsibilities to keep track of in their lives. They need a way to calm down and meditation is the solution. Successful people always find some time to meditate daily. They have a lot of work to do and staying calm and centered is the only way to function well.

Prayer and meditation will clear your mind of unnecessary thoughts that keep you worried and unfocused. Start by dedicating a fixed time to meditate daily and stick to it as much as possible. You can also make changes if necessary.

#5- They Are Focused On One Goal At A Time

If you read job descriptions and requirements, you are sure to find some that describe an ideal candidate as a 'multi-tasker.' If you scan a list of successful people, you will never encounter this description.

So, what is so bad about being a multitasker?

People who try to tackle a variety of tasks simultaneously are unable to focus completely. In contrast, successful people focus and work on one thing or one task at time. What should you do? Skip multitasking and instead, focus on one thing at a time. This ensures that each task is completed correctly and with excellence, which in the end saves time.

#6- They Are Chronic Readers

Successful people learn and get better with every passing day. Talk to any one of them and you will discover they are avid readers. From Apple's Steve Jobs and Microsoft's Bill Gates to Facebook's Mark Zuckerberg, everyone has their set of favorite books that they love to read and re-read.

Reading is the absolute best exercise for your mind. It keeps your mind alert and makes you informed about many topics. If you have not developed this habit yet, it is time to work on it. Aim to read a set number of books each month and stick to it.

#7- They Are People-Oriented

Businesses understand the power of communication and staying in touch with their customers and people around them. They realize that no matter how successful and wealthy they become; material wealth is fleeting.

People are focused on many things; they want to be wealthy or rack up achievements. To compete with others, they forget what is most precious to them: their family and friends. Successful people prioritize family and friends over material things.

#8- They Are Humble

Have you ever seen someone who is equally successful and arrogant? Successful people are usually not arrogant; they are humble and down to earth. They simply recognize their success is the product of their hard work, but they do not let it go to their heads.

They are thankful for what they have and respectful to everyone they encounter, regardless of their level of success. Many of them strongly believe in karma, in seed-time-harvest, they believe by doing good things, they will be rewarded with good things.

#9- They Are Persistent

Persistence is the single most needed and wanted quality to be successful and successful people have loads of it. Many people, especially the ones that are inventors and innovators, have high levels of persistence. They have managed to endure many obstacles and keep moving onward.

Persistence will keep you going whenever the situation is unfavorable or there are hardships. Successful people have gone through the wringer and know how to stay on their path. Start being persistent about achieving your goals and very soon you will have a new habit.

#10- They Are Self-Disciplined

If you have successfully incorporated all these habits but lack discipline, you will not be successful. Create discipline in your life. This is not strictly for people in the military; you can also benefit from it. Stick to these habits religiously and keep distractions at bay. It takes hard work and dedication to build habits, but it takes self-discipline to keep going.

Being successful should never be the only destination for any businessperson. It is just another achievement, to achieve greater, you should never stop learning and moving toward new goals in your life. You may come in this world looking like your parents, but you will leave looking like your habits. Our daily decisions are vital to our success.

Establish Joint Venture Partnerships

A joint venture is a business arrangement that is entered into by two or more parties on agreed terms. It is a beneficial way to run business and many businesses prefer a partnership instead of running it alone.

A joint venture is beneficial because all parties bring their skills and experience together on a single platform and divide the profit and loss equally based on the agreed percentages.

While joint ventures offer several advantages, they can be quite tricky and complicated to step into, therefore, it is important you calculate all the risks involved. To make sure that your joint venture partnership is successful, consider the following steps:

Before entering into business agreement with another party/parties, determine what is to be expected from each other. It may be an exciting experience but keeping things clear and legally documented will steer you clear from any possible conflicts. Everyone should follow a well-detailed business objective plan to determine what roles will be taken by each party.

Have a complete formal agreement of the venture to avoid any possible and future misunderstandings or conflicts. Add the financial contributions of each of the party, objectives, business structure, strategic operations, liabilities, the method of sharing loss and profit percentage, and everything else that is related to your business.

Before signing the papers, seek professional advice from your lawyer, accountant, and financial advisor. Tell them the reasons for the venture, your goals, method of achieving them and why have you chosen this route. It may sound time-consuming, but it will save you from future issues.

Do thorough research on all the partners joining you. Make sure they have an unblemished reputation because you will be publicly connected with one another. In the case of a poor partner, all your hard work and reputation will vanish. Therefore, take your time to search for the right partner.

The joint venture should have a governance policy to make strategic decisions. When there are more parties involved, things can get complicated. To counteract this situation, it is better to have a policy made in agreement with each member of the partnership.

Let's take a B2B BREAK right here.

Create a list of good habits that you want to practice:

_____
_____
_____
_____
_____
_____
_____

List who can hold you accountable to implementing these practices:

_____
_____
_____
_____
_____
_____

List 3 people you would love to do joint ventures with:

_____
_____
_____
_____

Create a plan/pitch for the type of event or business you would like to do with these individuals...

_____
_____
_____
_____
_____
_____

List the outcomes you would like to see because of these new practices:

_____
_____
_____
_____

Brand Stages

Lets' sum it up! Hopefully by now you have written notes all over your Brand To Bucks Guide and now have a clear view of your next steps. My goal is that you take time to answer the questions you never considered prior to picking up this book.

Having a plan is one thing, execution is another! Whether it took you a few weeks or months to process this information, the time of implementation is inevitable.

Here are a few of the major stages I walk my clients thru when launching a product or service:

> *Concept to Creation* – Research, research, research! This is the early stage of brand development. Here we create a road map to birthing the big idea!
> *Time of Testing* – Putting the brand on trial in small groups to see how it delivers the brand promise. This can take months or years depending on the product or service.

- *Soft Launch* – Gathering the influencers. Getting the service or product to groups of influencers that can attest to the quality of the brand.
- *Official Launch* – It's go time! Use all the data to develop the content for marketing. Get your products and services out to the masses.
- *Serve for a Fee* – Impact as many people as possible. Some of my clients get so fearful when they hear the word "sell", so I tell them just "serve" for a fee.
- *Review* – Check and measure the results. What are people saying? What is the brand impact?
- *Evolve* – Change, Shift, Adjust, GROW!
- *Repeat* – Take it back to Step 1! What's next? What's new? How else can the brand serve its customers and remain in scope of the brand mission?

These eight steps can take months and in most cases years. Each one requires a different set of skills and strategy, so take your time, be patient. *It is not an overnight process!*

Use this guide as a reference, a source to go back to as you apply each level to the development of your brand. Feel free to contact me, if you are a woman in business reading this join our CEO Chick Network. Surround yourself with like-minded individuals who understand this entrepreneurial journey. You CAN DO this!

Your Notes

Brand To Bucks

Brand To Bucks

Brand To Bucks

Brand To Bucks

Client Stories

I hope the stories and information in this Brand To Bucks guide has bought you both clarity and courage! These are some foundational tools to get your brand off to a good start and to see your earnings increase. Building a successful brand is not an overnight process. It requires everything we discussed and more! Brand to Bucks is a reference tool to help you walk through your entrepreneurial journey. This portion of the book provides a few visuals of my work.

It is my passion to help entrepreneurs and organizations create content that brings their brand identity to life. Your images, videos, and written content must have the ability to pull people in. Your goal is to find a way to disrupt the market and have all eyes on you.

Websites

Before anyone buys your products or services, they will google you! Trust me your website and social media pages will be what makes or breaks a deal for potential customers and/or organizations interested in doing business with you. Your home page should reflect your brand promise. Avoid using too many words but focus on the imagery, movement, video, sound, functionality and the ability to convert visitors to paying clients.

VERONICA
FIGUEROA
RE/MAX
Real Estate Is About YOU.

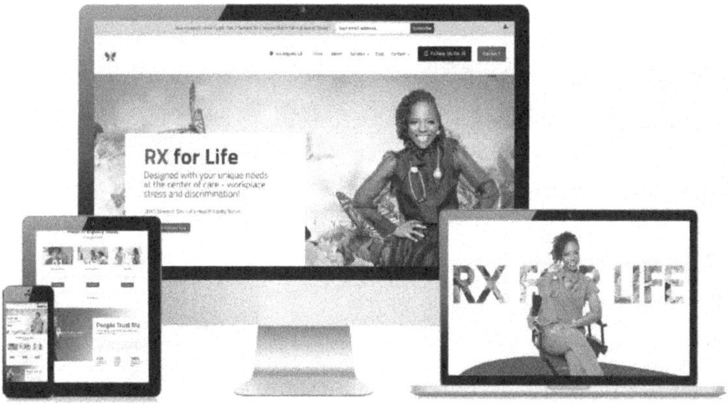
RX for Life
Designed with your unique needs at the center of care - workspace stress and discrimination!
People Trust Me

Book Covers

More and more are becoming authors! Books are powerful tools that last a lifetime, they give readers more insight into your way of thinking and living.

They are like business cards on steroids! I have had the pleasure of working with clients that write their own material as well as others that hire professional ghost writers.

Regardless of your skill sets, your story can be transformed into a book. The cover must give potential customers a feel for what the book is about and attract customers to pick it up. Whether it is inspirational, romantic, fictional, non-fictional, transformational, spiritual, educational, or a how to guide, be sure to engage the audience. Your book should add value even if it is entertaining.

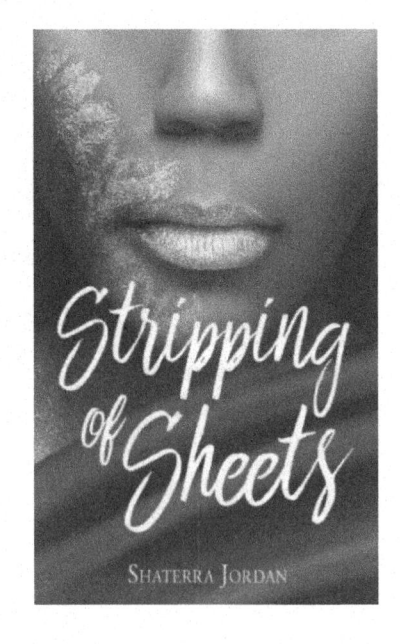

Logos

Your logo is your stamp; it is the image that delivers the promise of your brand. I love to combine text and a picture or icon (graphic representation) in a logo.

They can be used together or separately depending on the marketing approach. The Successfully Equipped logo utilizes what I call, the finish line ring image or the text. The Alandus D. Sims logo can be used with just the text or the image of the lion medal. Creating logos with several dimensions is necessary in my book and provides a brand with options for various purposes.

Images

With smart phones and increased access to cameras everyone may think for a second, they are a photographer. When hiring someone to build your brand, you have to do your research.

Find out their work history, are they just starting out? How does their brand look?

My client Shaterra Jordan hired someone months prior to meeting me to work on her brand. She requested a photo shoot that would depict her Stripping of Sheets brand and the outcome was the image on the left. When she showed me the source of her inspiration, I immediately noted the difference of the first attempt and assured her I could get it done. The shoot was so successful; the images are amazing! The after photo is just one example of what we were able to create using the sheet concept she desired!

Before   After

In totality, I have provided information, experience, examples, and how to's. This book is your guide to building your brand. Remember building a brand takes time, clarity, meditation, research, trial, and error. Be patient with yourself! Stay the course and finish STRONG!

What Clients Are Saying

"In business you will run across what I like to call BRANDING BOSSES. They have a type of BRANDING gift that will help you change your life. They help you really believe that you can do GREAT things in this world! BRANDING BOSSES help you reach out and use the right keys that God has given you to unlock doors that have been waiting for you to walk through. I am proud to say that Coleen Otero is THE BRANDING BOSS in my life!" - Author Shaterra Jordan | Kissimmee, FL

"Coleen has a gift to bring your ideas to life! Her creativity and laser focus on delivering her best is second to none. Don't look any further if you want to elevate your brand and stand out in the crowd" - Michele Wiggins | Orlando, FL

"Coleen Otero gives you all the wisdom and insight to orchestrate your business into a profitable success! Branding with Coleen led me to a profit rebound! She is the best!" - Jacqueline Griffith | Queens, NY.

"I met Coleen Otero at the right time! I knew it was time for me to brand my business; Virtuous-Tees, but with so many options, I did not know where to start. She was very patient, friendly, and professional with me. Coleen helped me believe in my vision even when I did not see the full picture. She helped me get to the end results in each goal I set. The website creation was amazing! She knew what I wanted even when I could not put into words. She pointed me in the right direction and provided resources necessary to become successful. After hiring Coleen as my branding coach my second income increased a whopping 800%! She truly has a passion to see women in business succeed!!!"- Kenya Thomas | Atlanta, GA

About The Author

Celebrity Hair and Makeup Artist, Branding Strategist, Mentor, Motivational Speaker, Author, Entrepreneur, Wife, and Mom to 4 boys and a stepdaughter, Coleen Otero is the definition of doing it all with STYLE! With more than 20 years of experience in the Beauty Industry, Coleen has dedicated her life to not only helping individuals to look beautiful on the outside but feel beautiful on the inside.

Whether working on set or speaking on stage Coleen Otero openly shares her lessons learned as an entrepreneur, mom, wife, and woman of faith. Her life's passion is to assist her clients in being their best! From leading her women in business network, **CEO Chicks** to branding seminars and workshops; let's not forget her fun and fabulous hair extensions line, Pure Luxe... her resume speaks for itself!

This Beauty & Branding Expert's work and products have been featured on networks like **Bravo, BET, NBC, FOX, CBS, WE TV** and more. Her VIP Clientele is filled with community leaders, CEO's, entertainers like **Sherri Shephard** from the View, **Sisaundra Lewis** from the Voice, **Myesha Chaney** from Preachers of LA, **Junice Rockman** from Relationship Rescue and Bravo's Thicker Than Water. Coleen was the 2018 Lead Hair Stylist for talent featured on **BET's Black Girls Rock** Marketing Campaign, directed by Alan Ferguson and Hosted by Queen Latifah.

Her success story has been featured in **The Huffington Post**, **The Orlando Business Journal** and several times on **Fox 35**. As the Founder and CEO of YourBeautyXpert, LLC (Y.BE.X), Coleen is not just satisfied with being an expert in her field, but she is passionate about teaching others to become successful as well! She and her team of industry professionals develop what she calls "iCandy" marketing strategies for her branding clients.

With services ranging from video promos, photo shoots, website development, logos, product line concepts, production, social media management and more! She's talented, transparent, and in her Brand To Bucks 30 Day Virtual E-Series, she freely shares the solutions and strategies she has learned on her road to success! Coleen is on a mission to help her clients walk in their God given purpose with style, while creating a brand that is unforgettable!